Georges Seurat Makes A Point

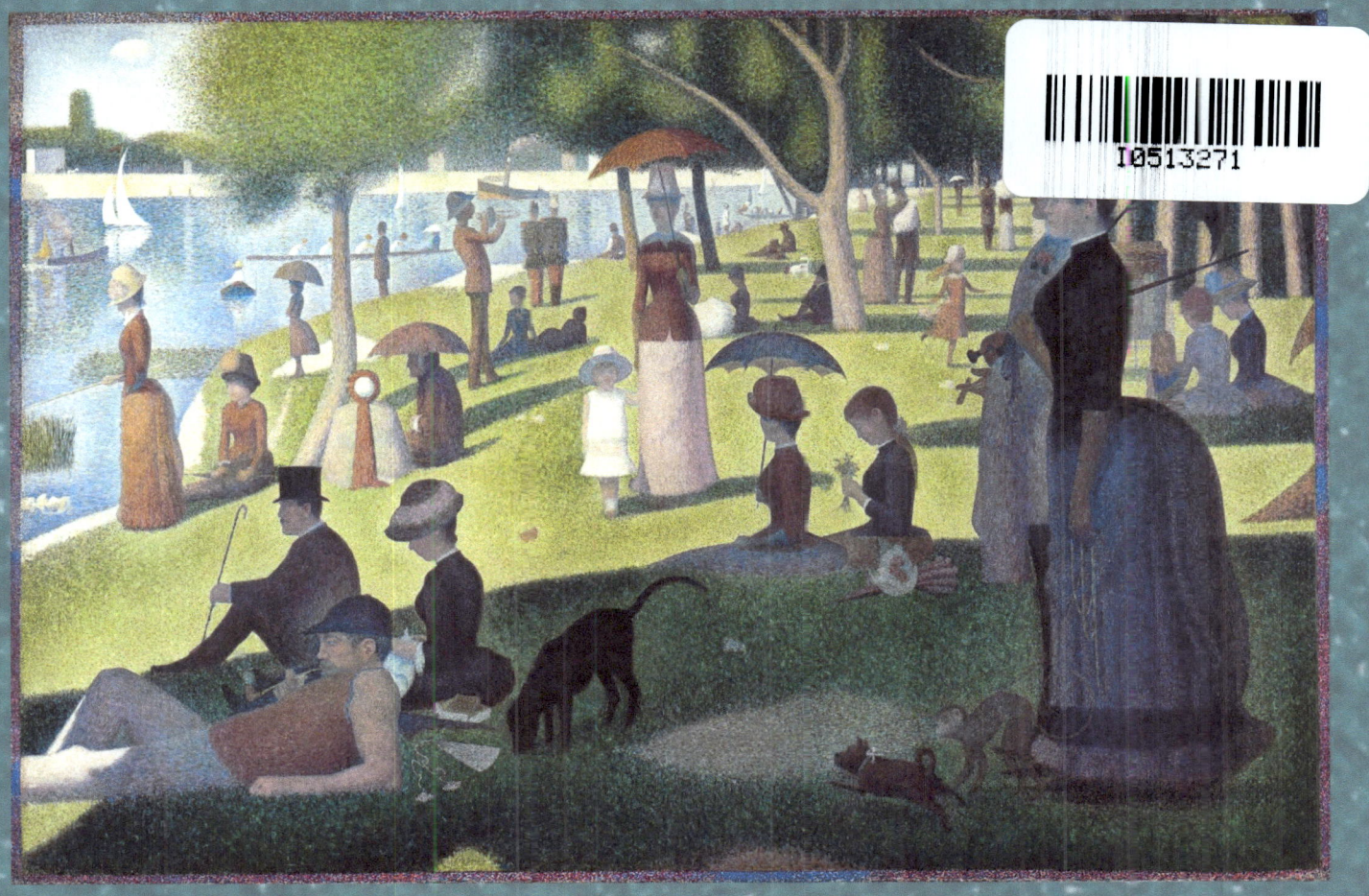

by Mrs. Keriotis' Kindergarten
with help from Grayce Beaver, Zoey Kazmarski,
and Ava Smith

Dedicated to children who can find new worlds in classic works of art.

Text by Mrs. Kelli Keriotis, her 2019-20 Kindergarten class, with help from Grayce Beaver, Zoey Kazmarski, and Ava Smith

Image Permissions: The images used of the Seurat paintings are public domain used for educational purposes.

Image of Georges Seurat was created by Gary Golkin *Georges Seurat 2014©* color pencil, oil pastels on paper www.garygolkin.com/seurat-index used with permission.

Stippled pictures were created with the software a popular free online photo editor in Japan. https://www.photo-kako.com/en/pointillism.cgi

Copyright © 2020 by Grow a Generation

All rights reserved. This book or any portion thereof may not be reproduced or used in any manner whatsoever without the express written permission of the publisher except for the use of brief quotations in a book review or scholarly journal.

ISBN 978-1-71601-937-1 Grow a Generation

Sewickley, PA 15143
www.growageneration.com

Any royalties earned from the sale of this book are donated to We Charities.

Mrs. Keriotis' Kindergarten class was enjoying some quiet reading time.

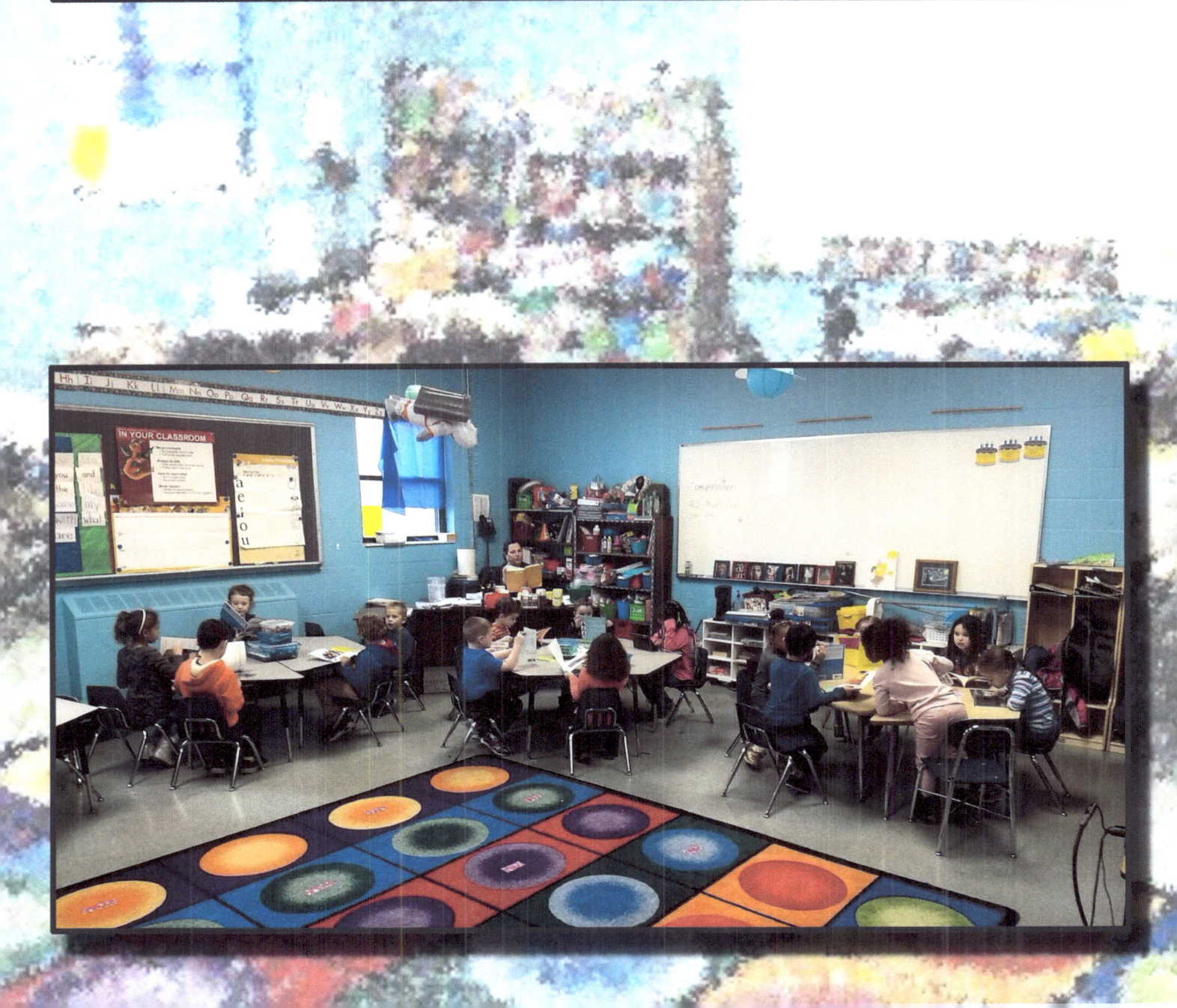

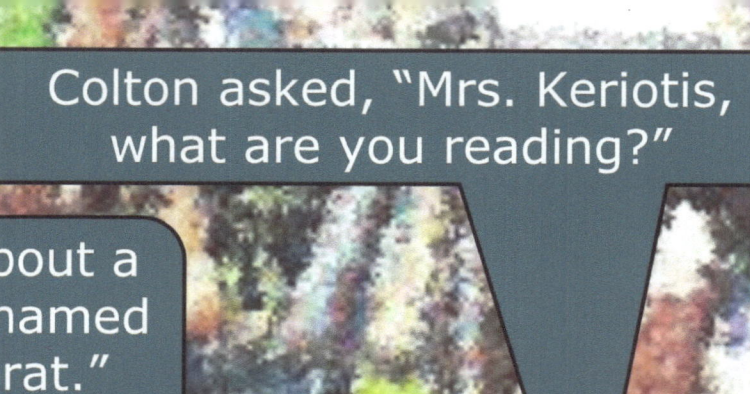
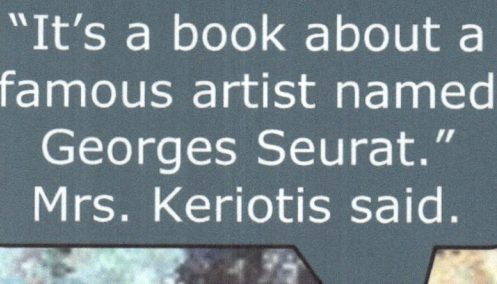

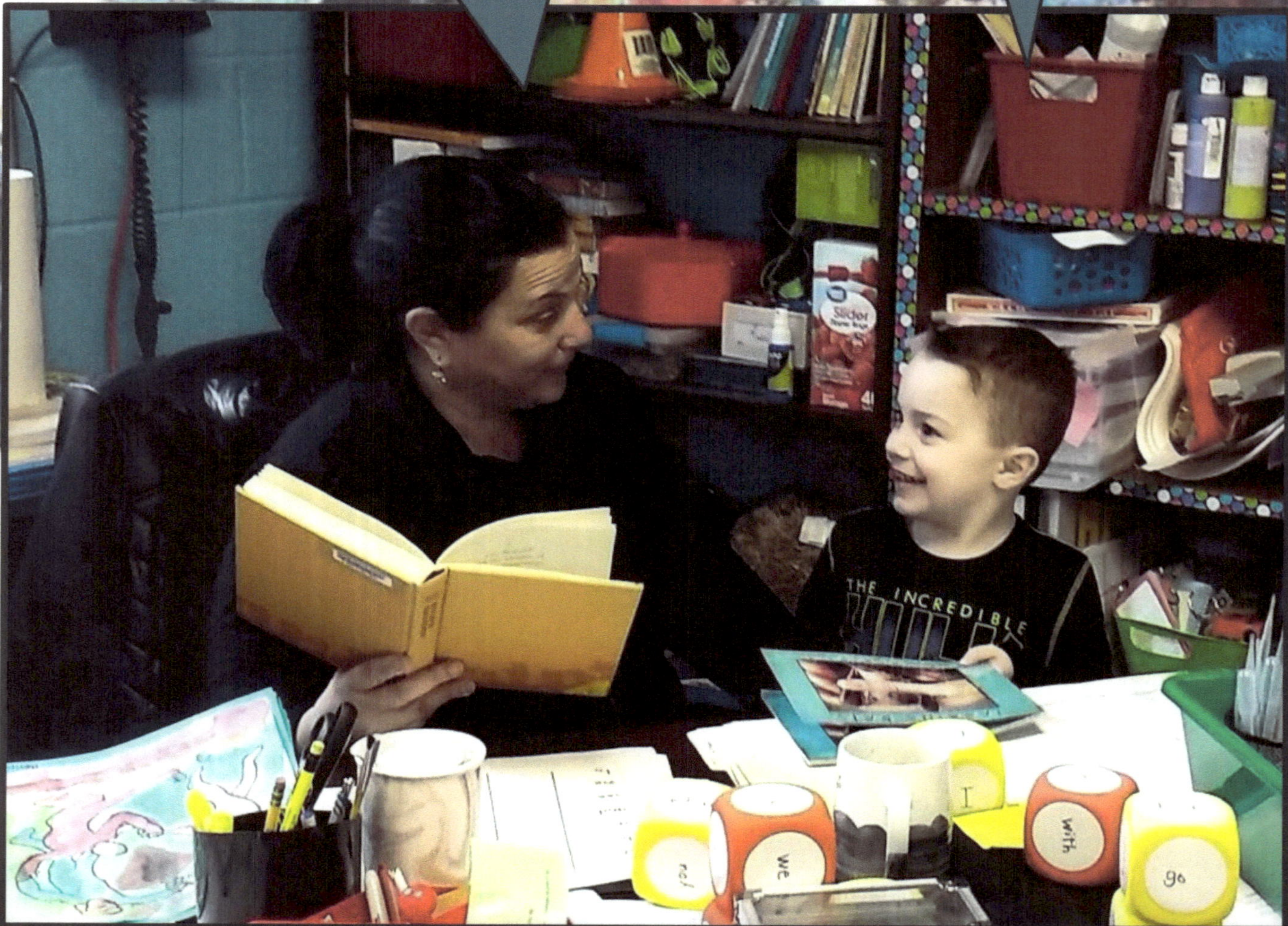

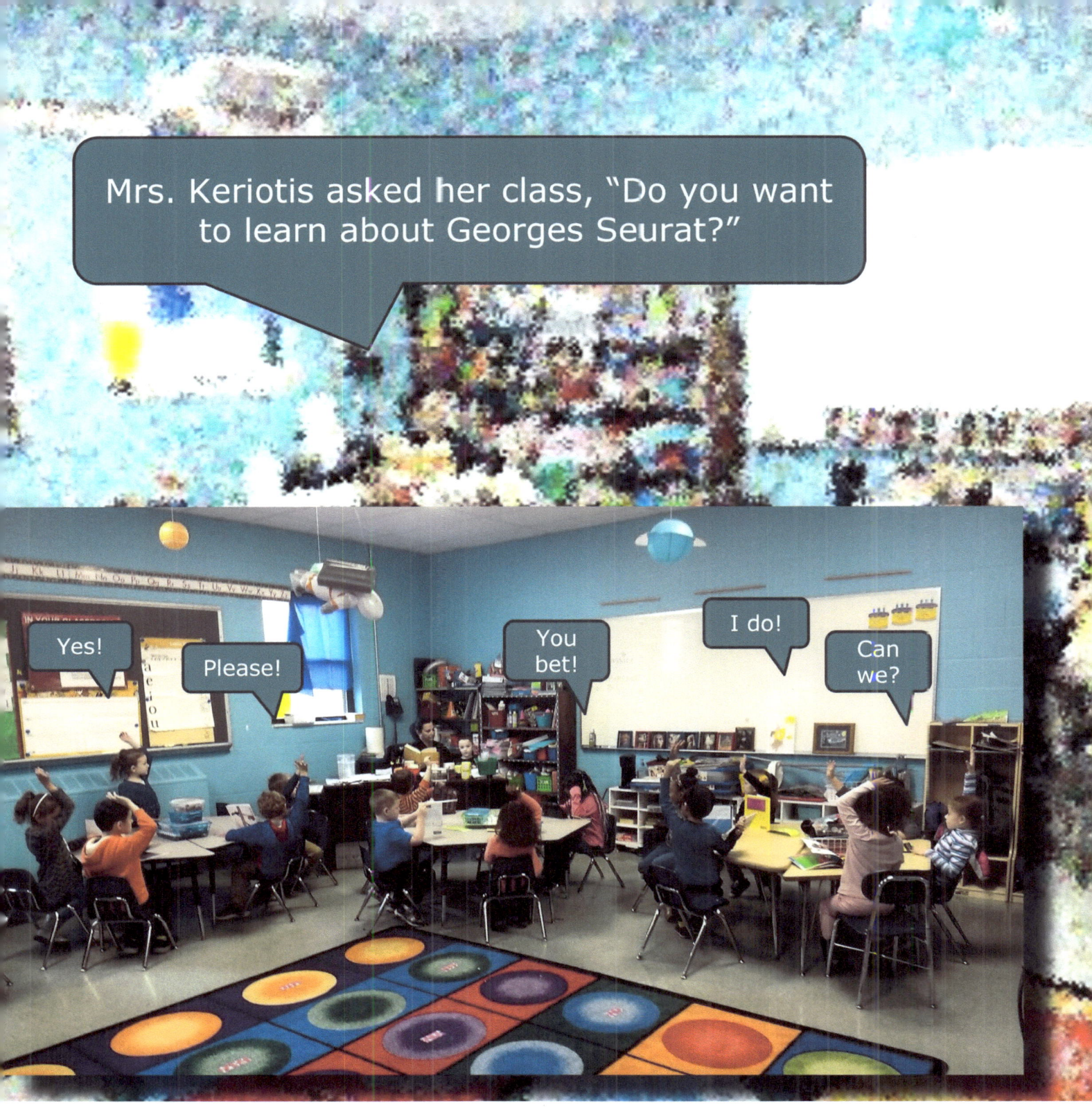

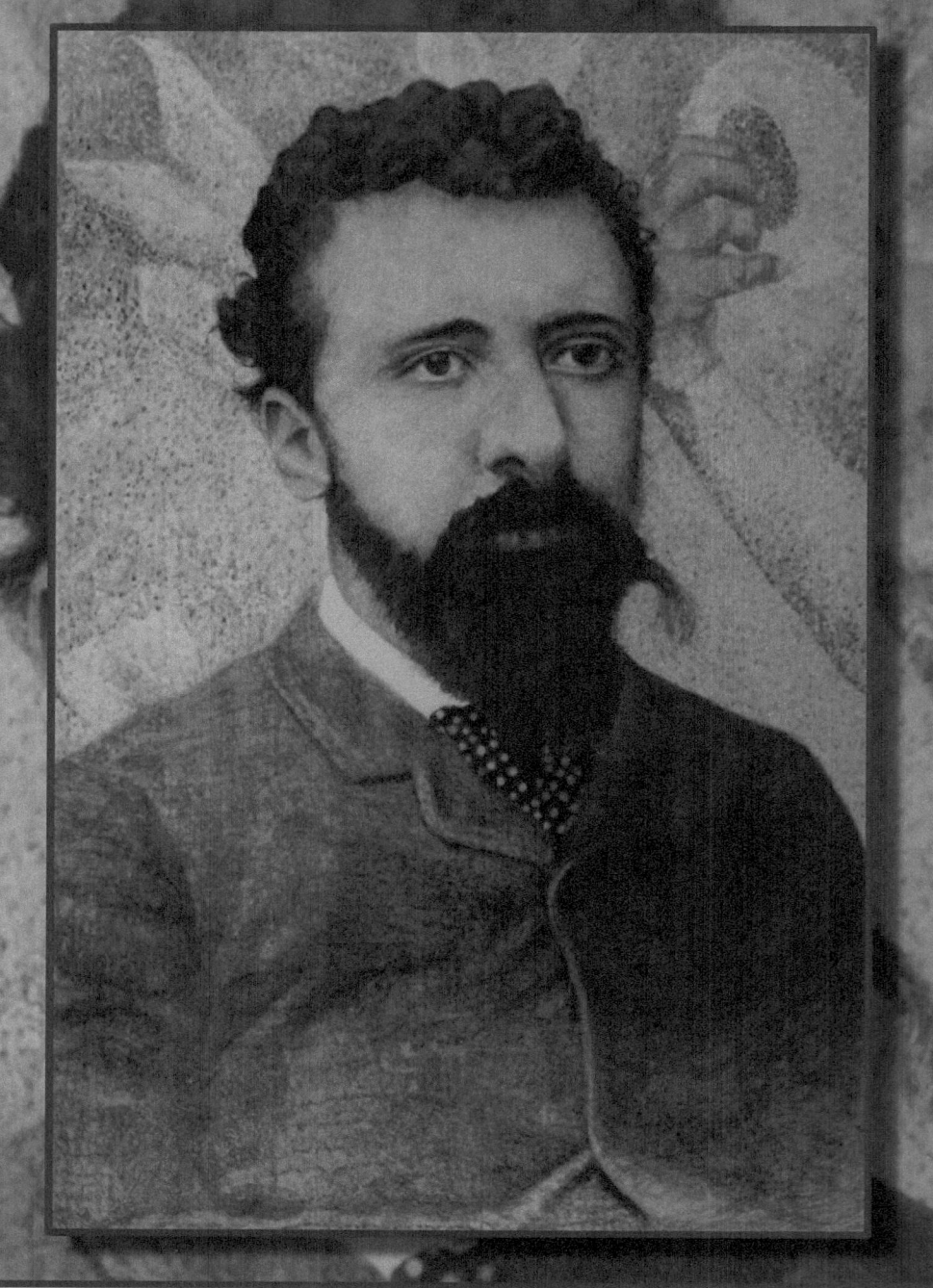

Georges Seurat was an artist who lived over a hundred years ago.

He was born in France, and he lived there most of his life. France is in Europe. Can you find France on the map of the world?

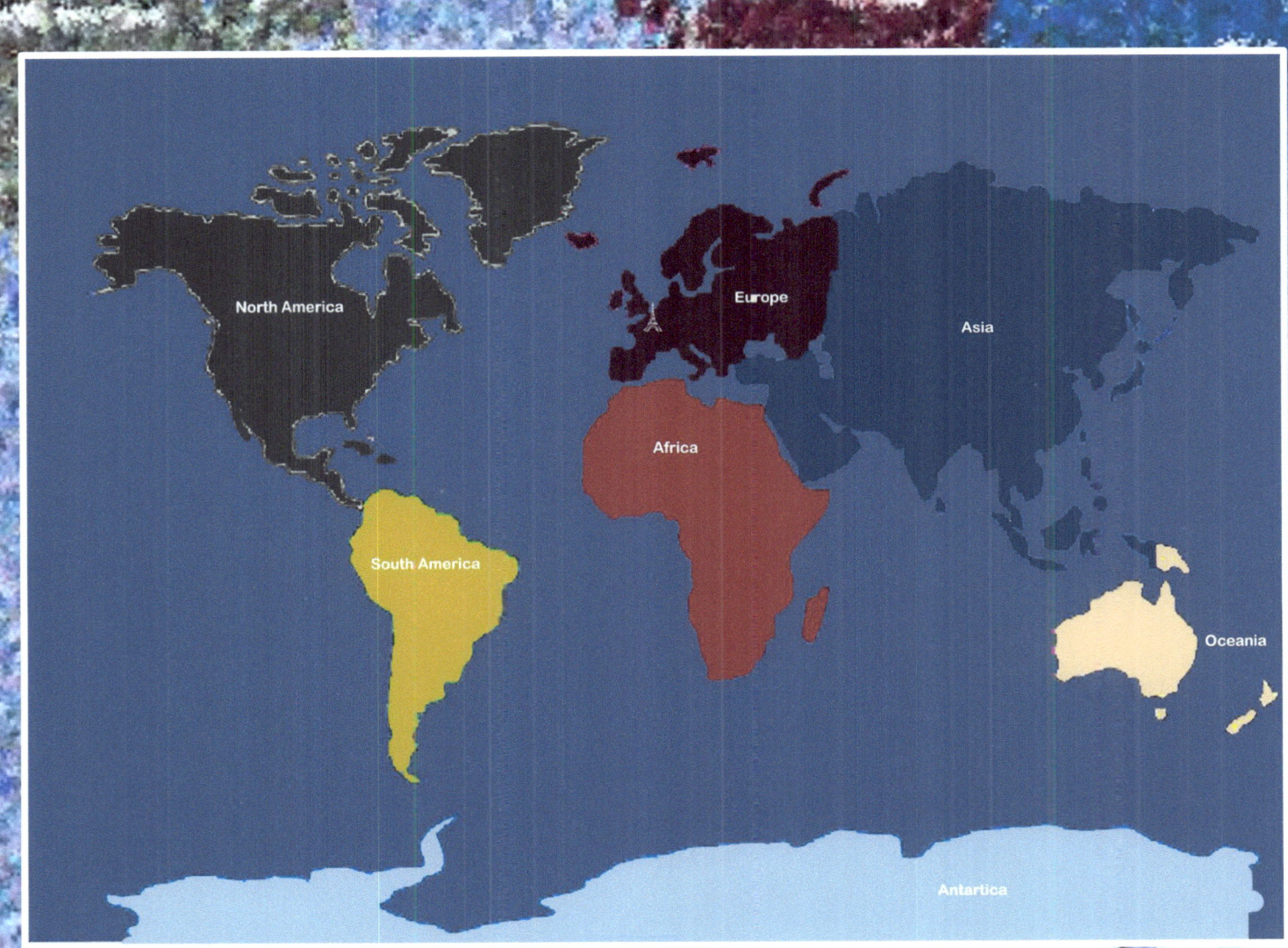

Georges liked painting pictures of Paris. The Eiffel Tower is in Paris.

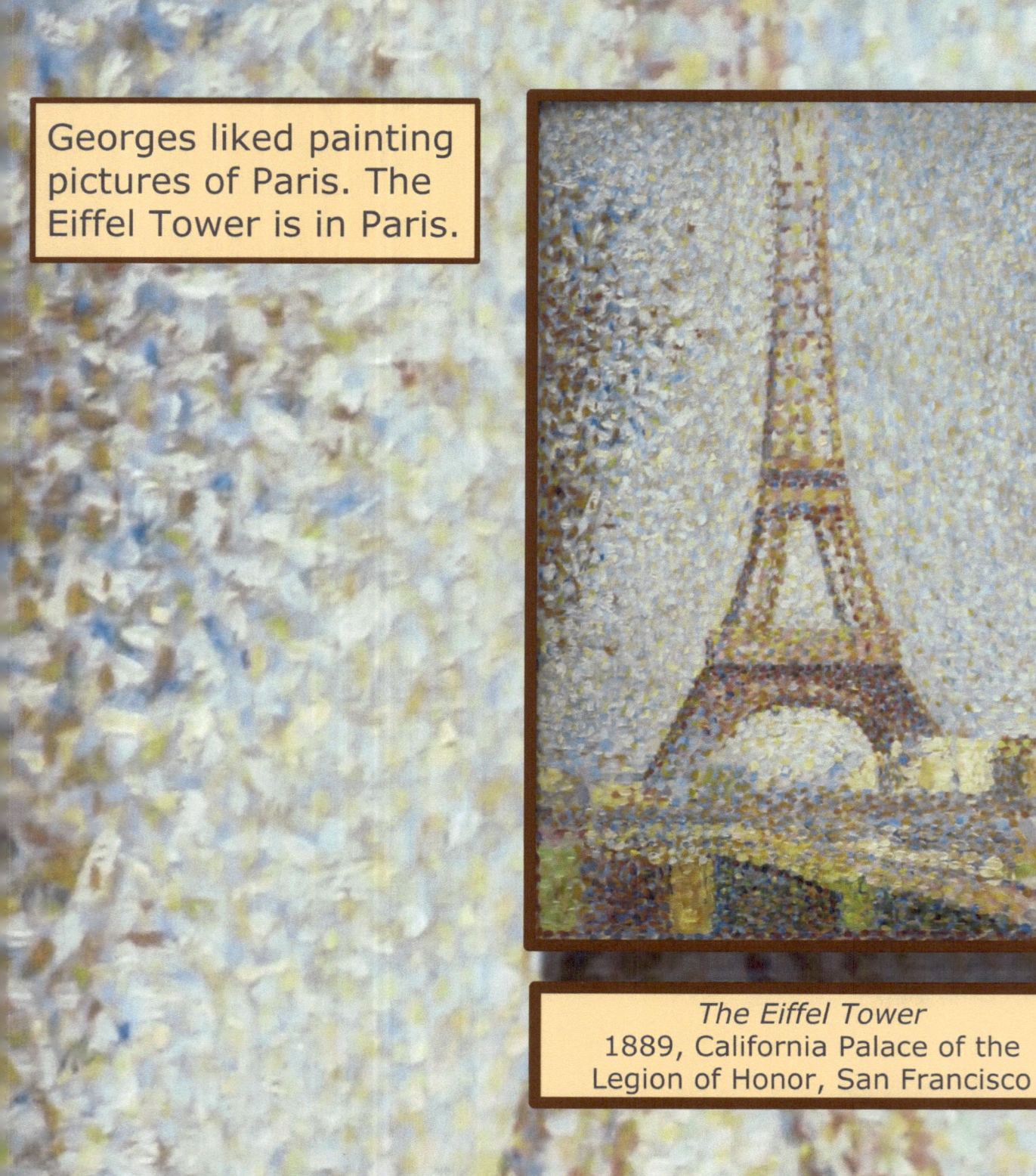

The Eiffel Tower
1889, California Palace of the Legion of Honor, San Francisco

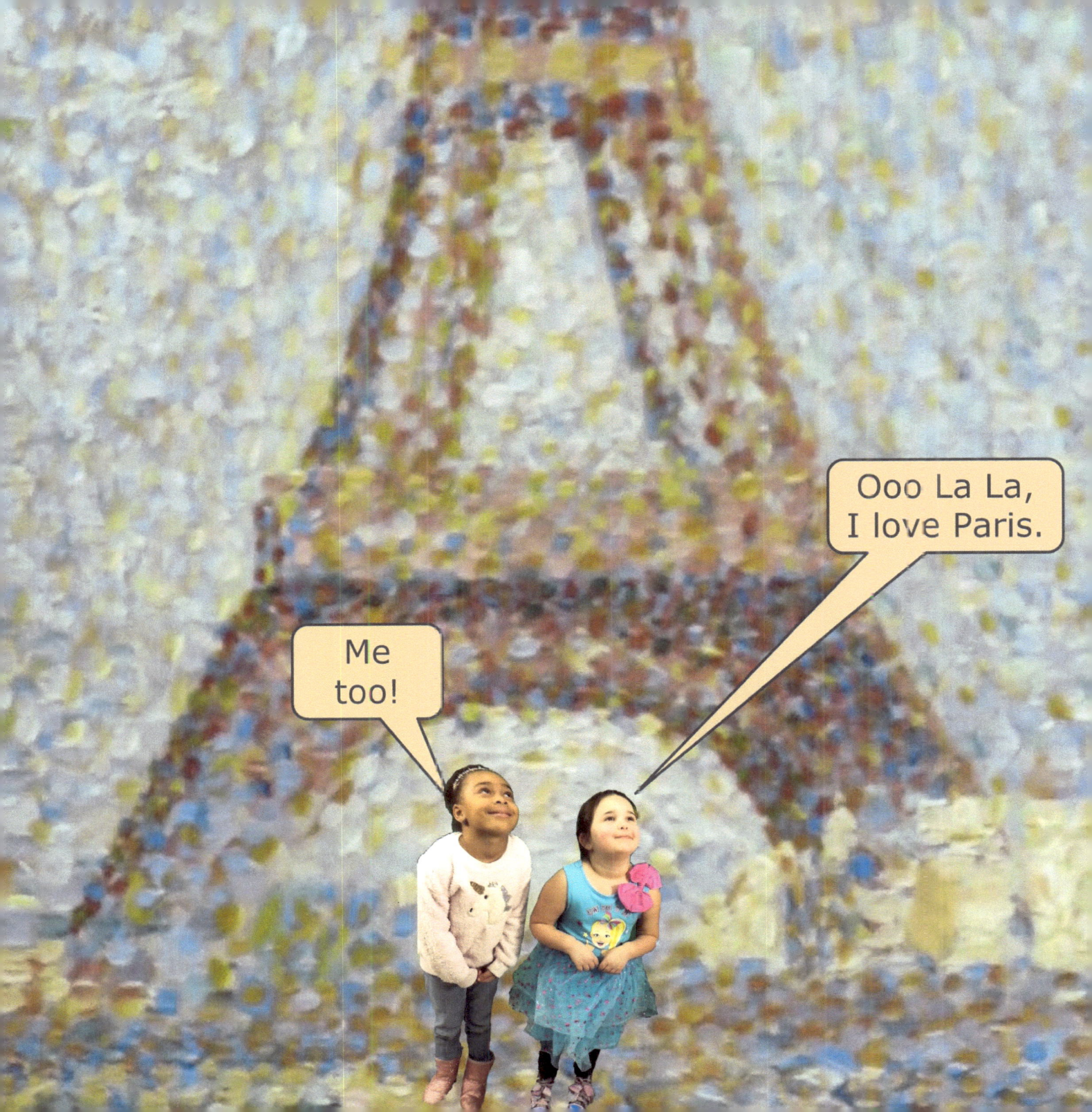

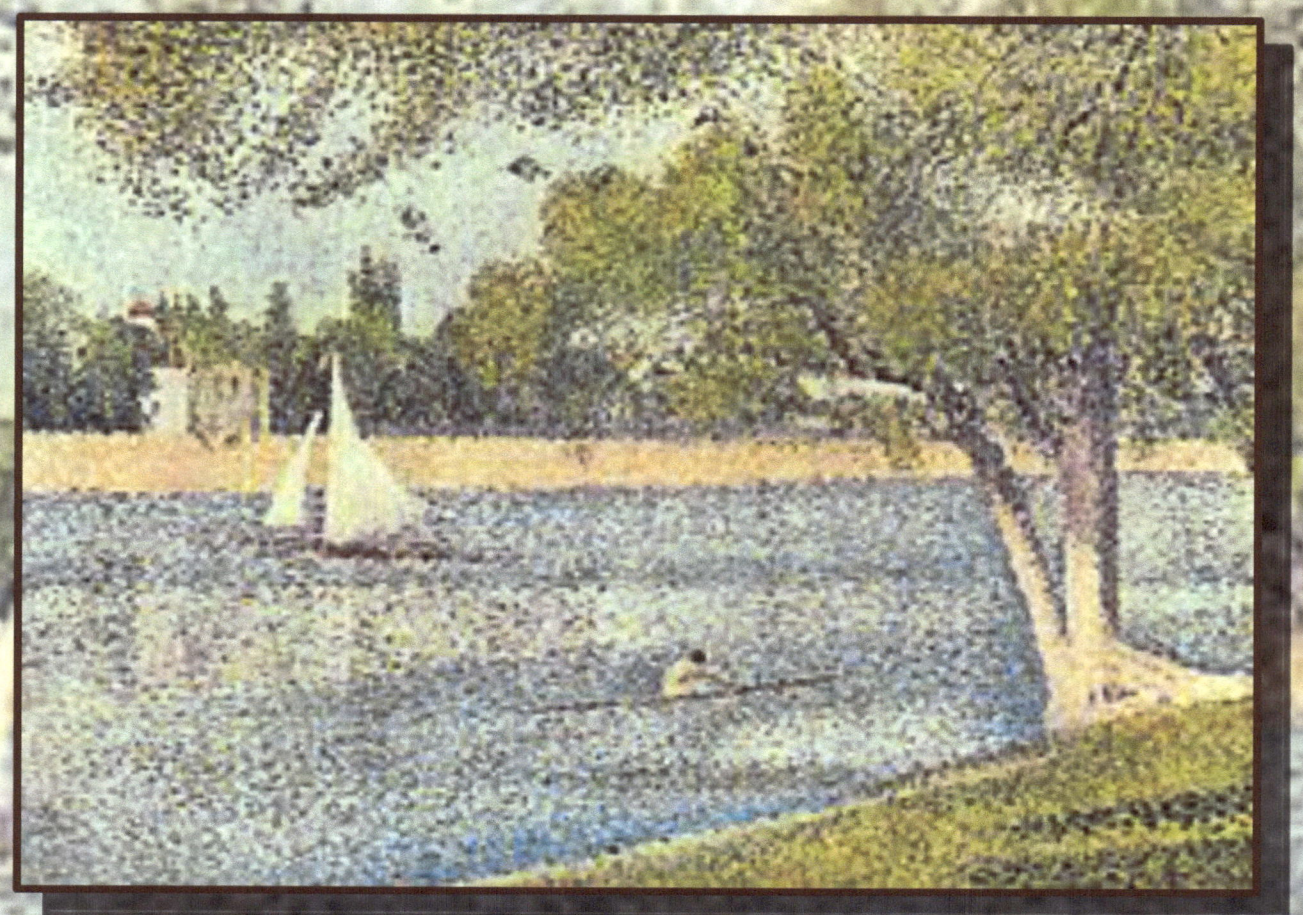

The Seine and la Grande Jatte – Springtime
1888, Royal Museums of Fine Arts of Belgium

Paris has a beautiful river called the Seine. The river flows through the heart of Paris.

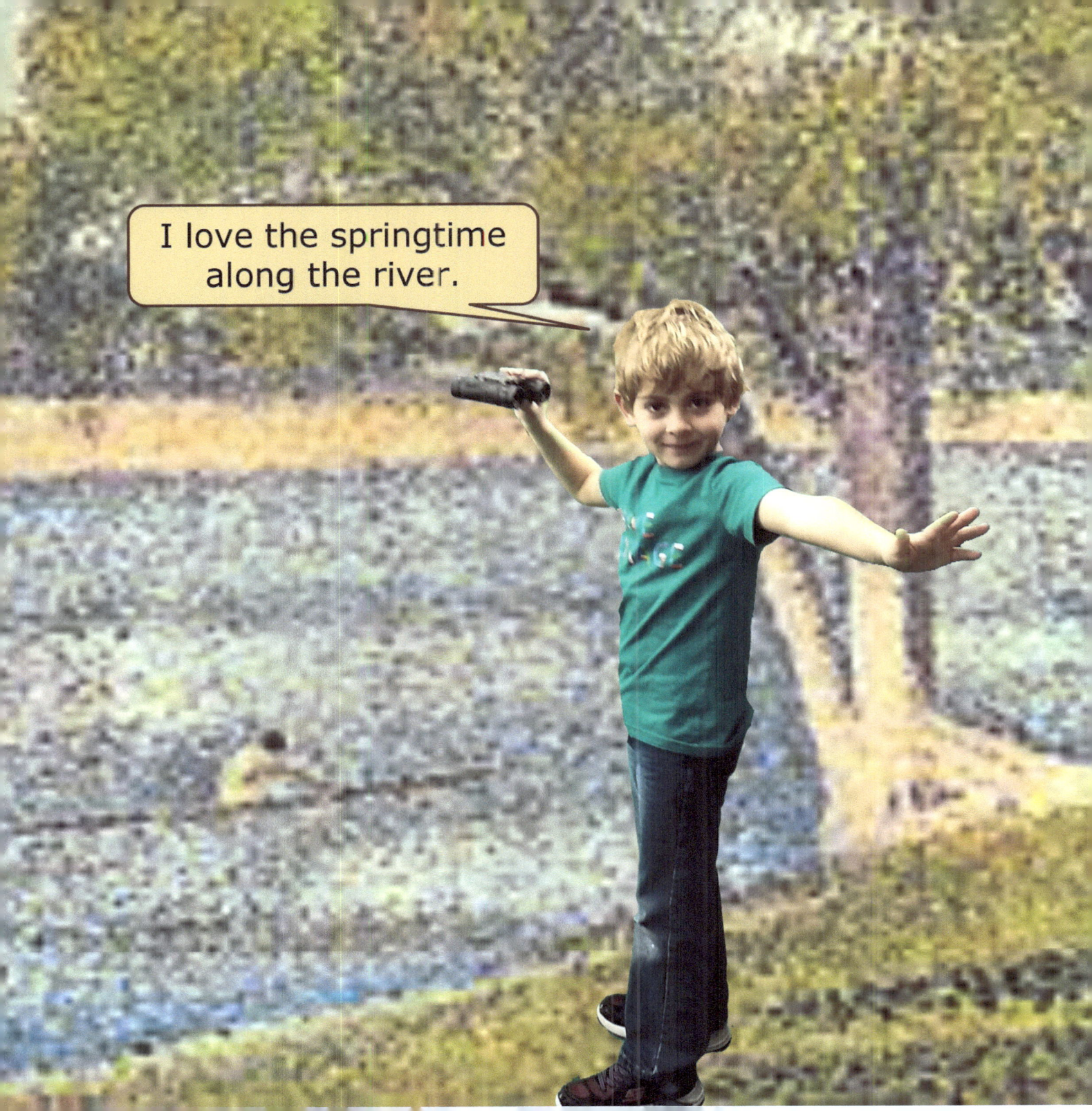

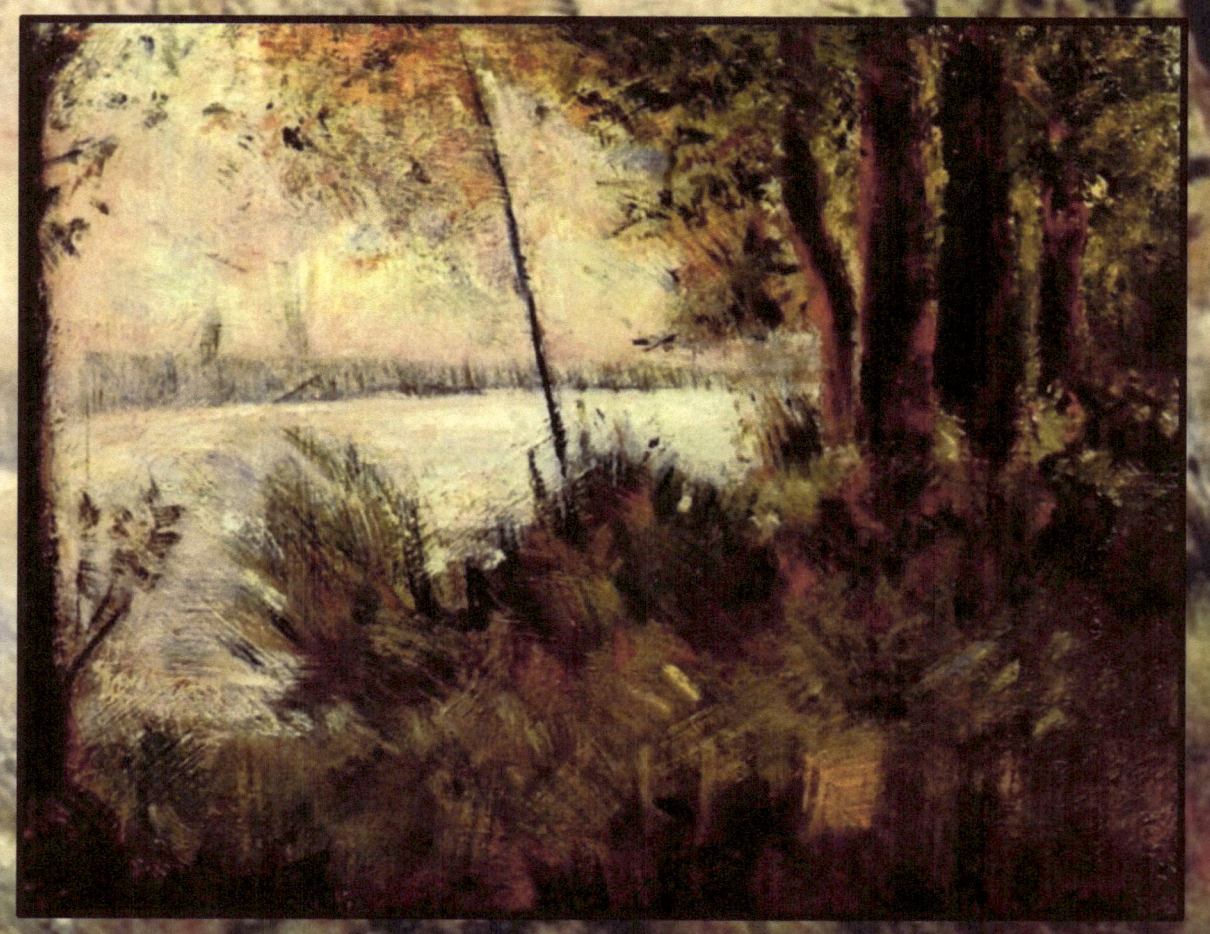

Overgrown Slope
1881, Dallas Museum of Art

Georges would find a place to sit near the river then slowly add a dot at a time to the canvas. The dots combined to paint a picture of the water and its overgrown banks.

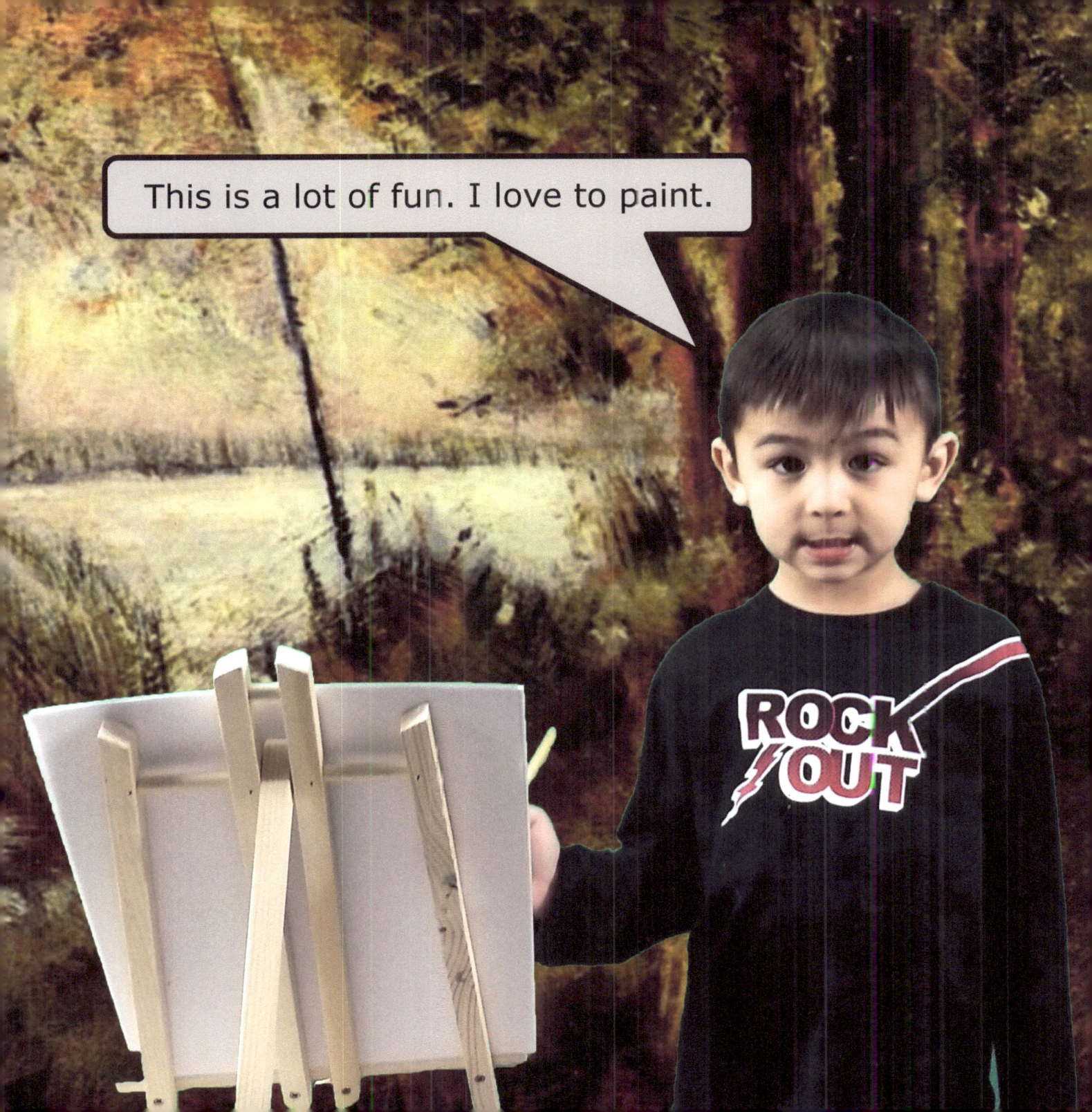

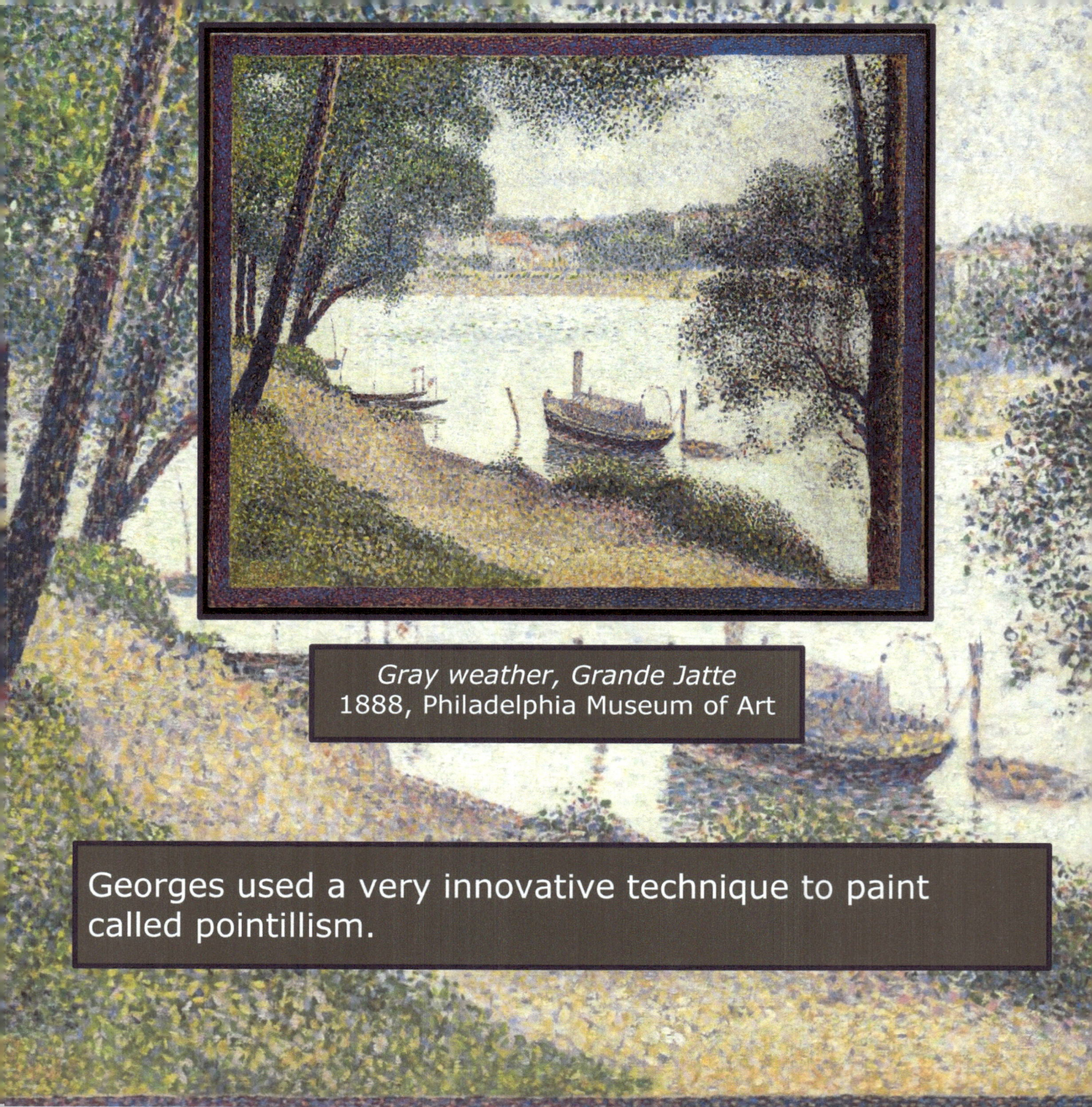

Gray weather, Grande Jatte
1888, Philadelphia Museum of Art

Georges used a very innovative technique to paint called pointillism.

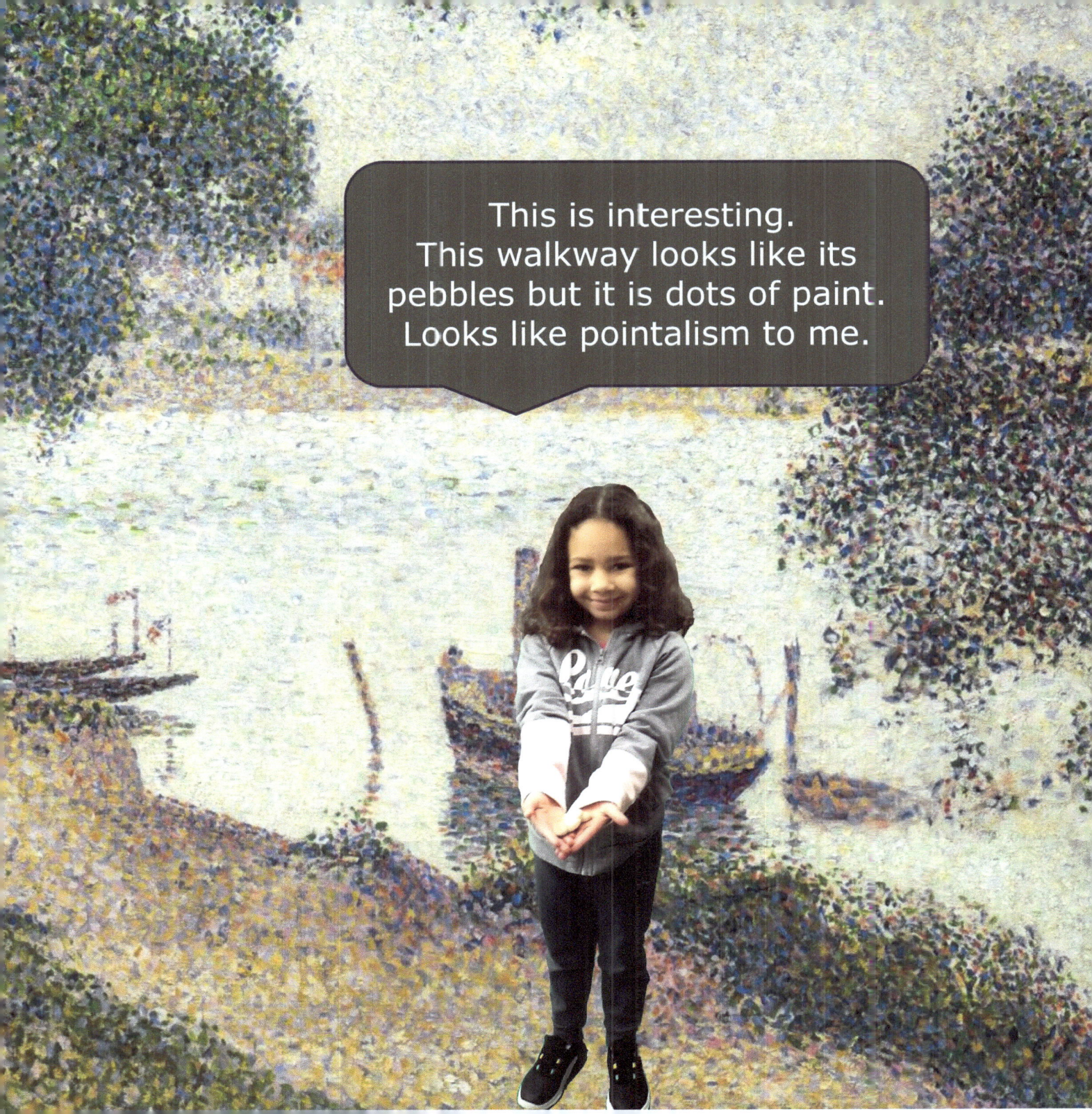

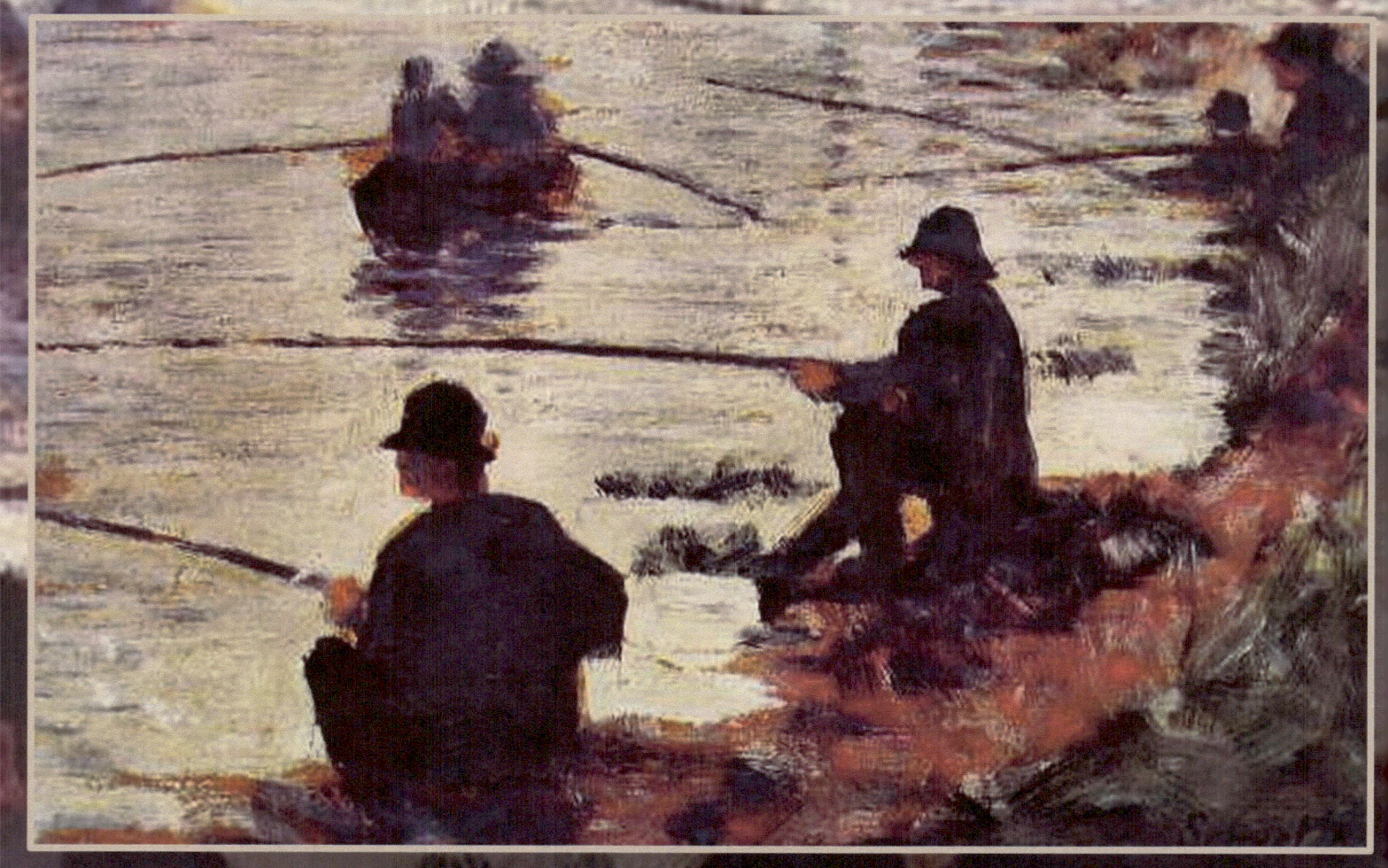

Fishing in The Seine
1883, Musée d'art moderne de Troyes

The Seine River was thriving with life. Even today people fish from its banks near Paris.

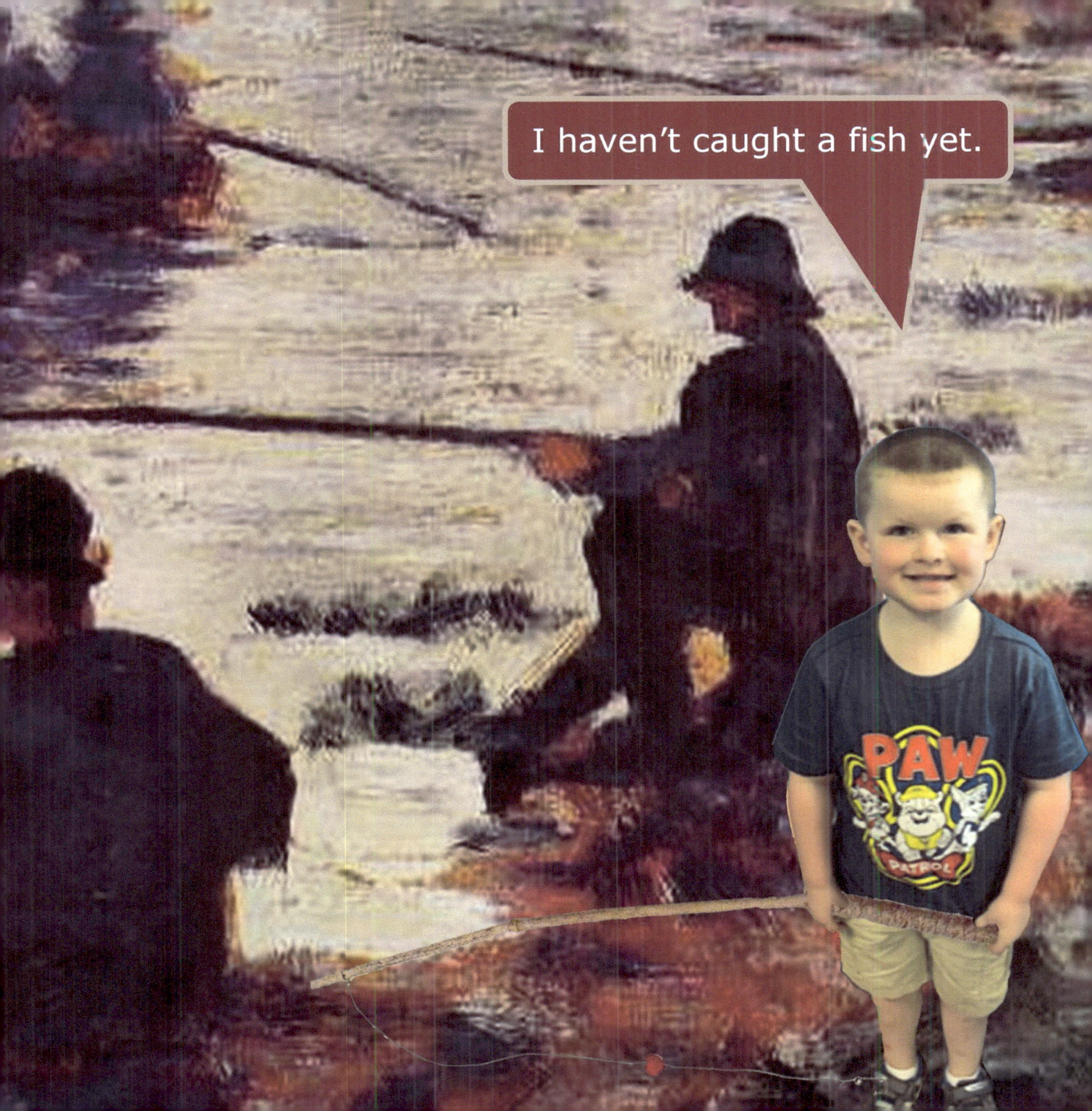

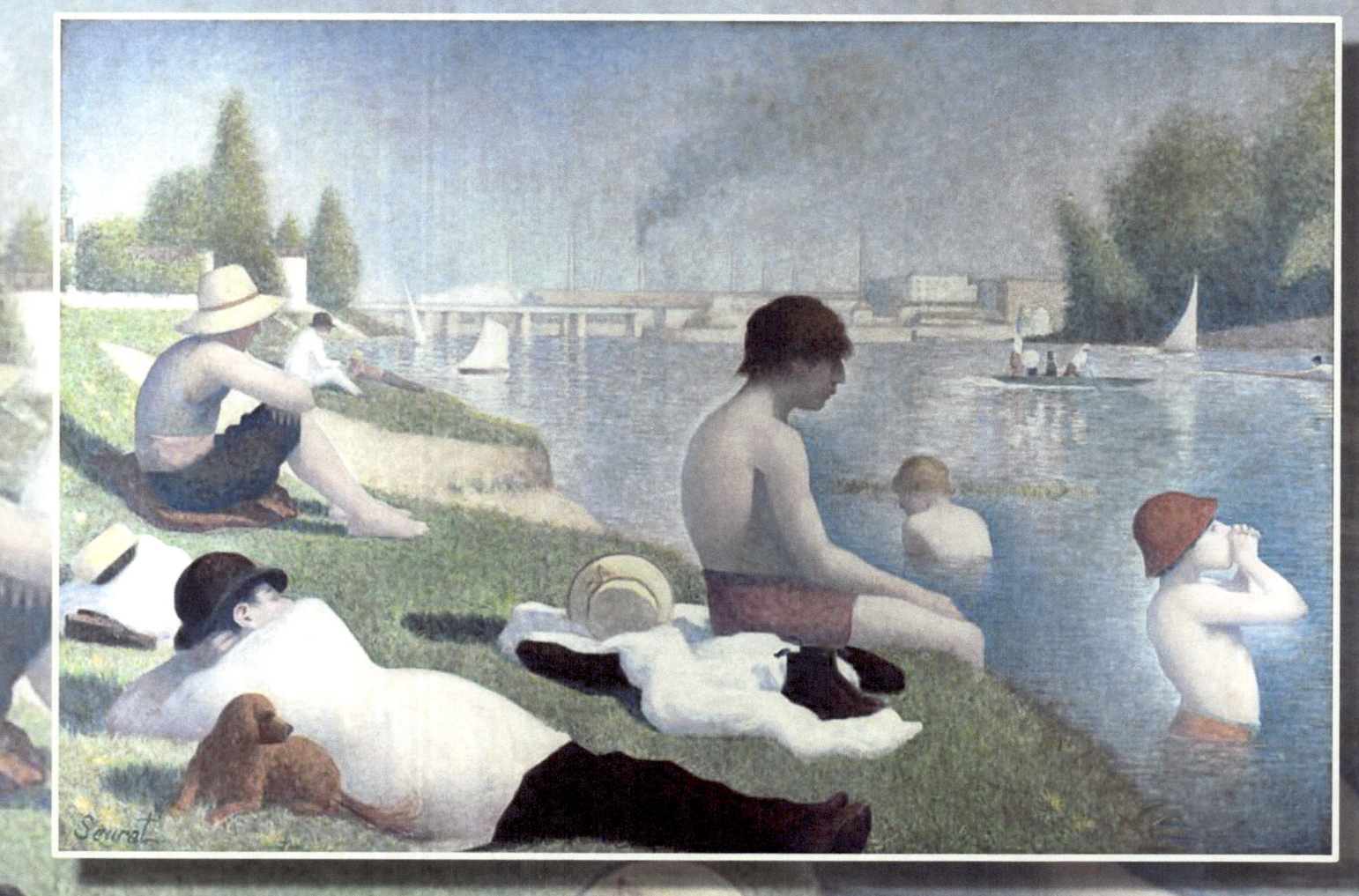

Bathers at Asnières
1884, National Gallery, London

Georges was really good at using brush strokes from his paintbrush to create a sense of timelessness.

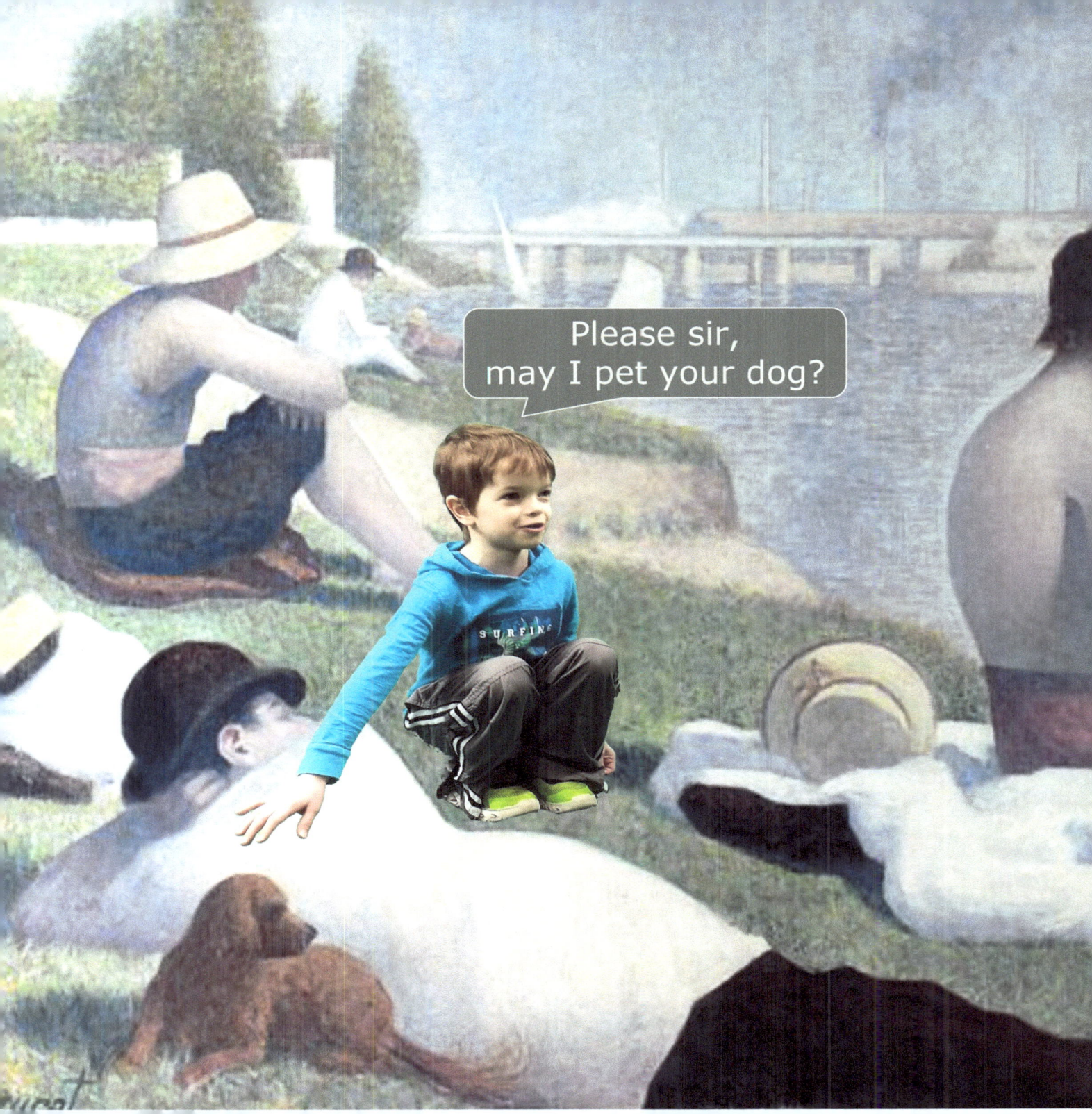

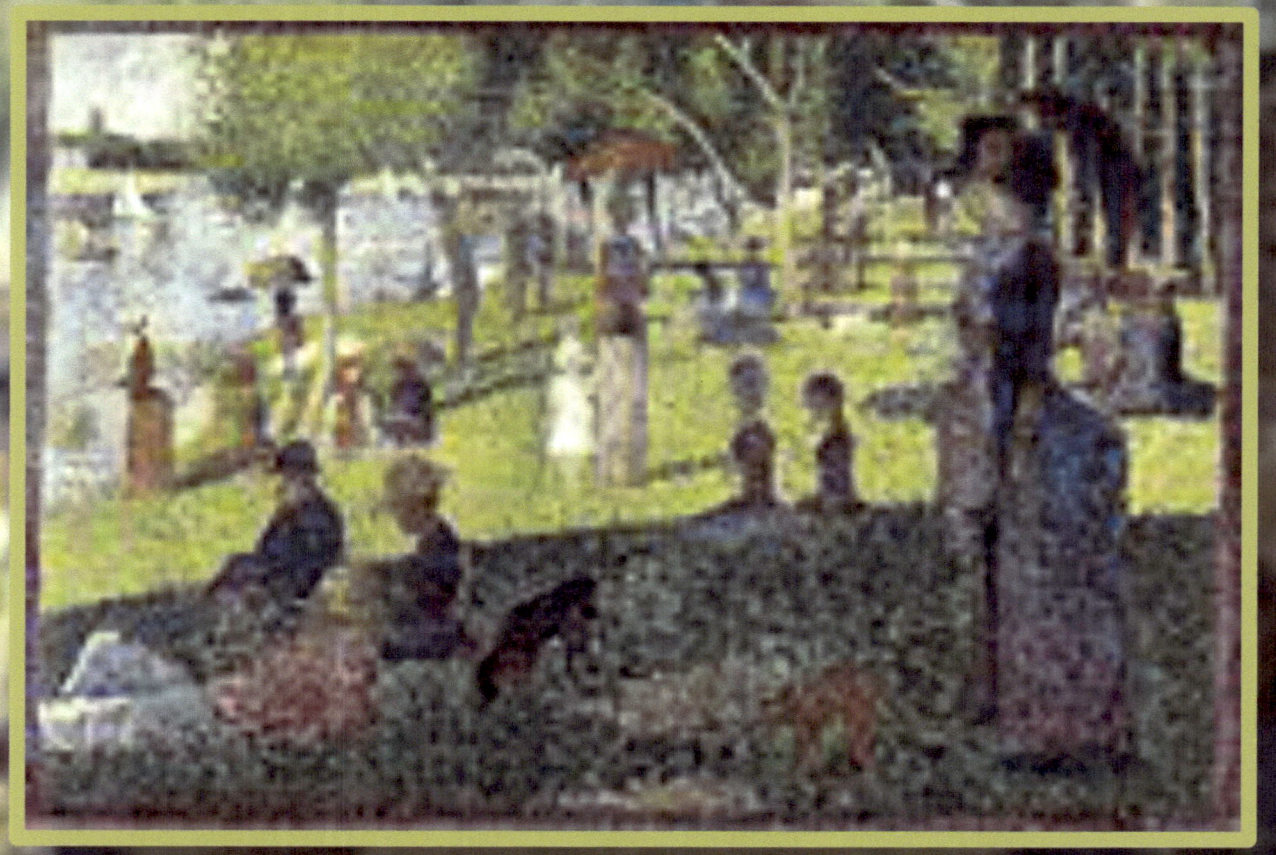

Study for A Sunday Afternoon on the Island of La Grande Jatte
1884–85, Metropolitan Museum of Art, New York

This is his most famous painting. He made several sketches first. The painting took many months. Georges saw painting as a very exact science which blended colors to create a more luminous picture.

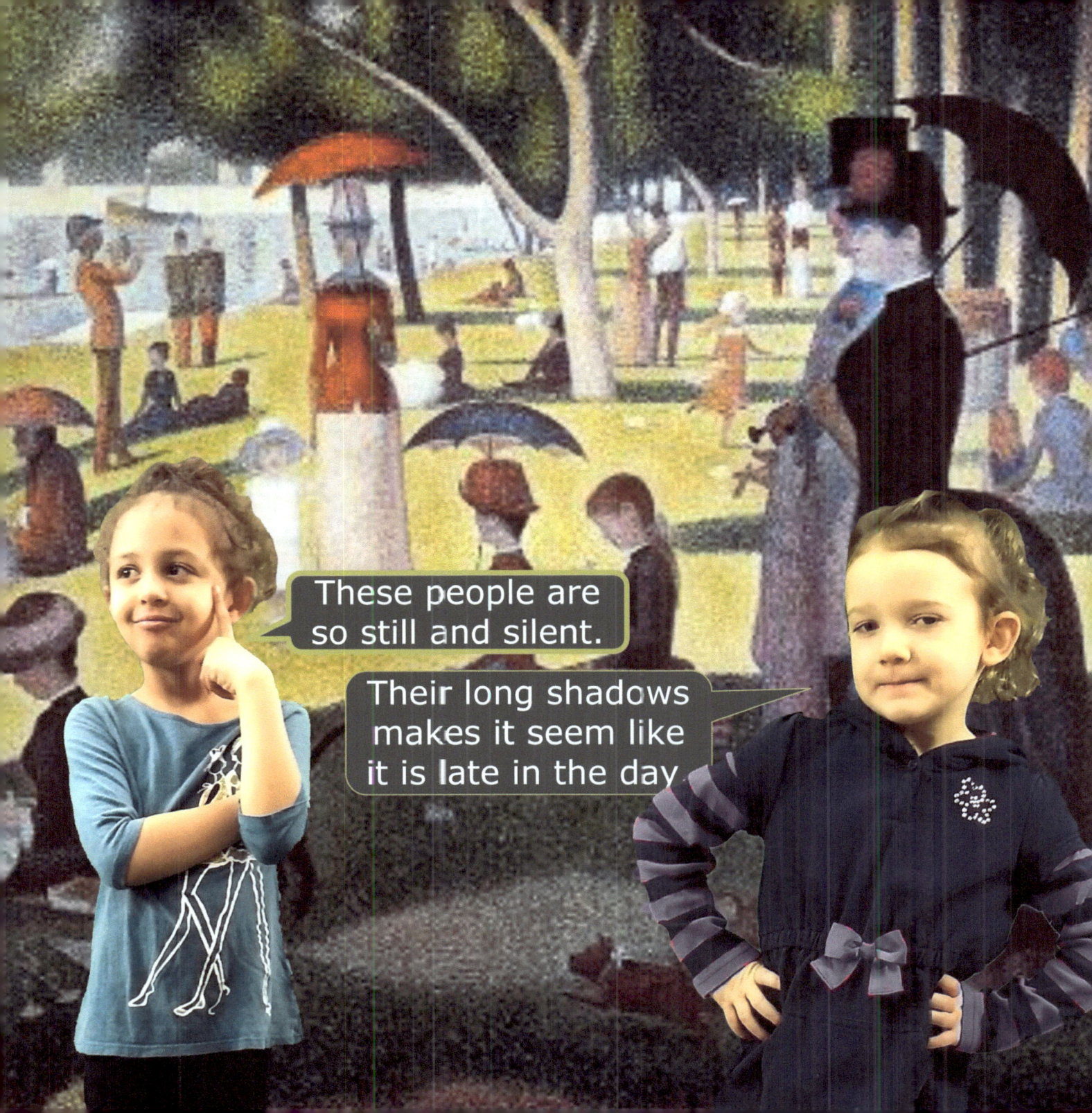

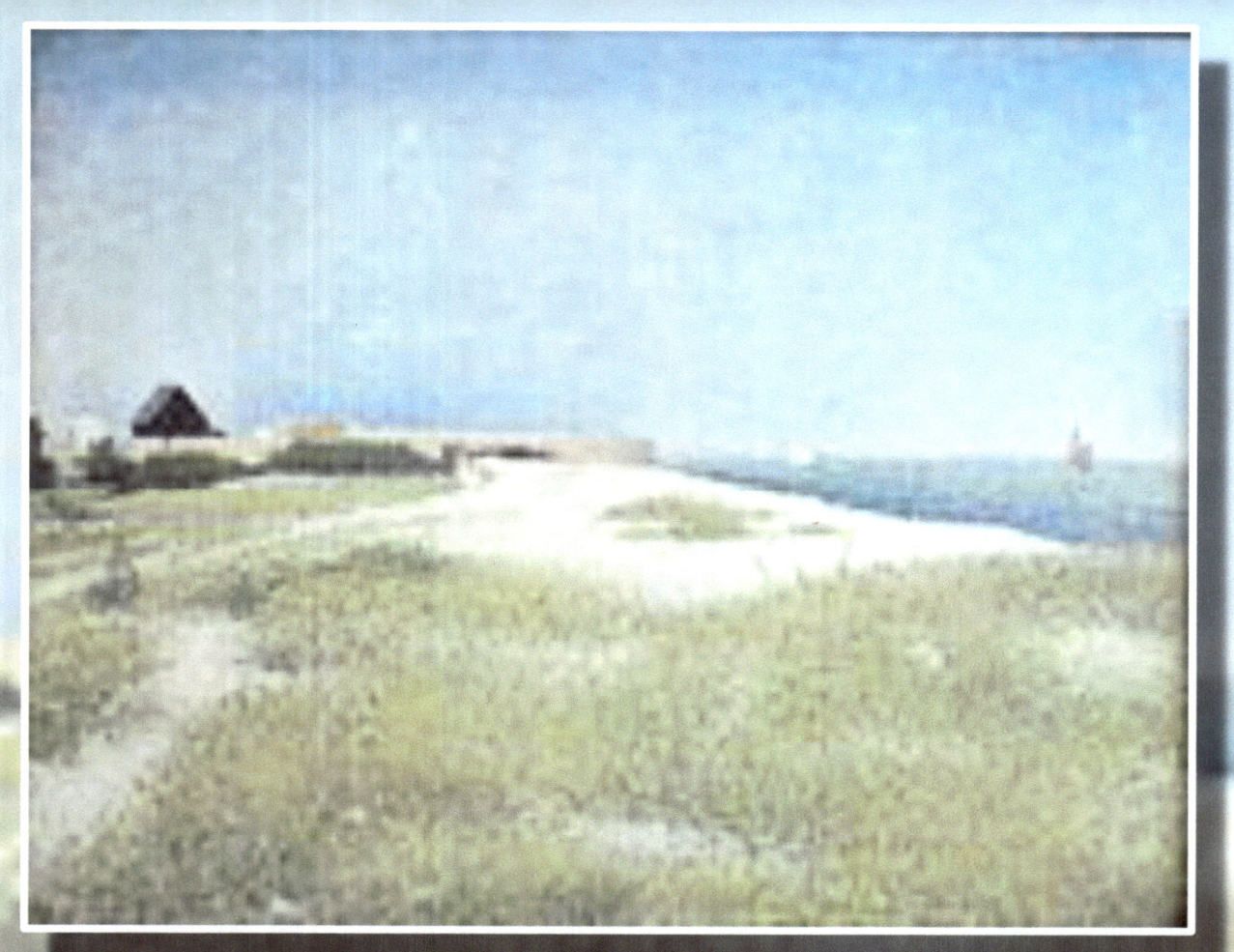

View of Fort Samson
1885, Hermitage Museum, St. Petersburg

Pointillism is when you use a lot of little dots to mix colors on the canvas instead of on the pallet.

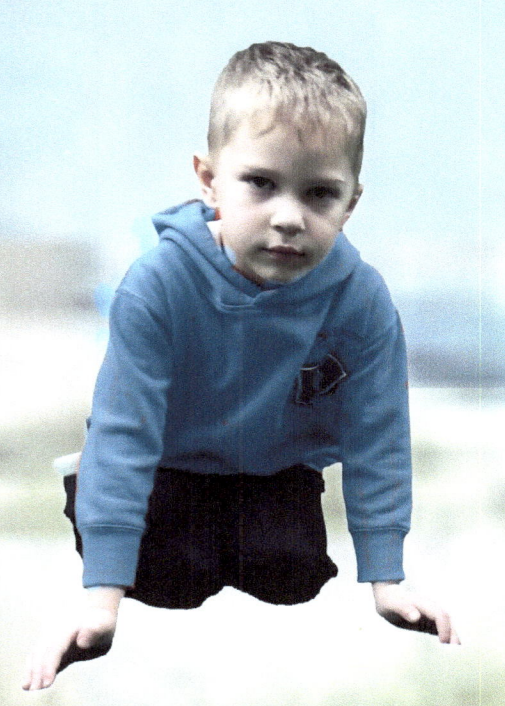

> These are colors made by combining dots of color. This is amazing, almost like grains of sand.

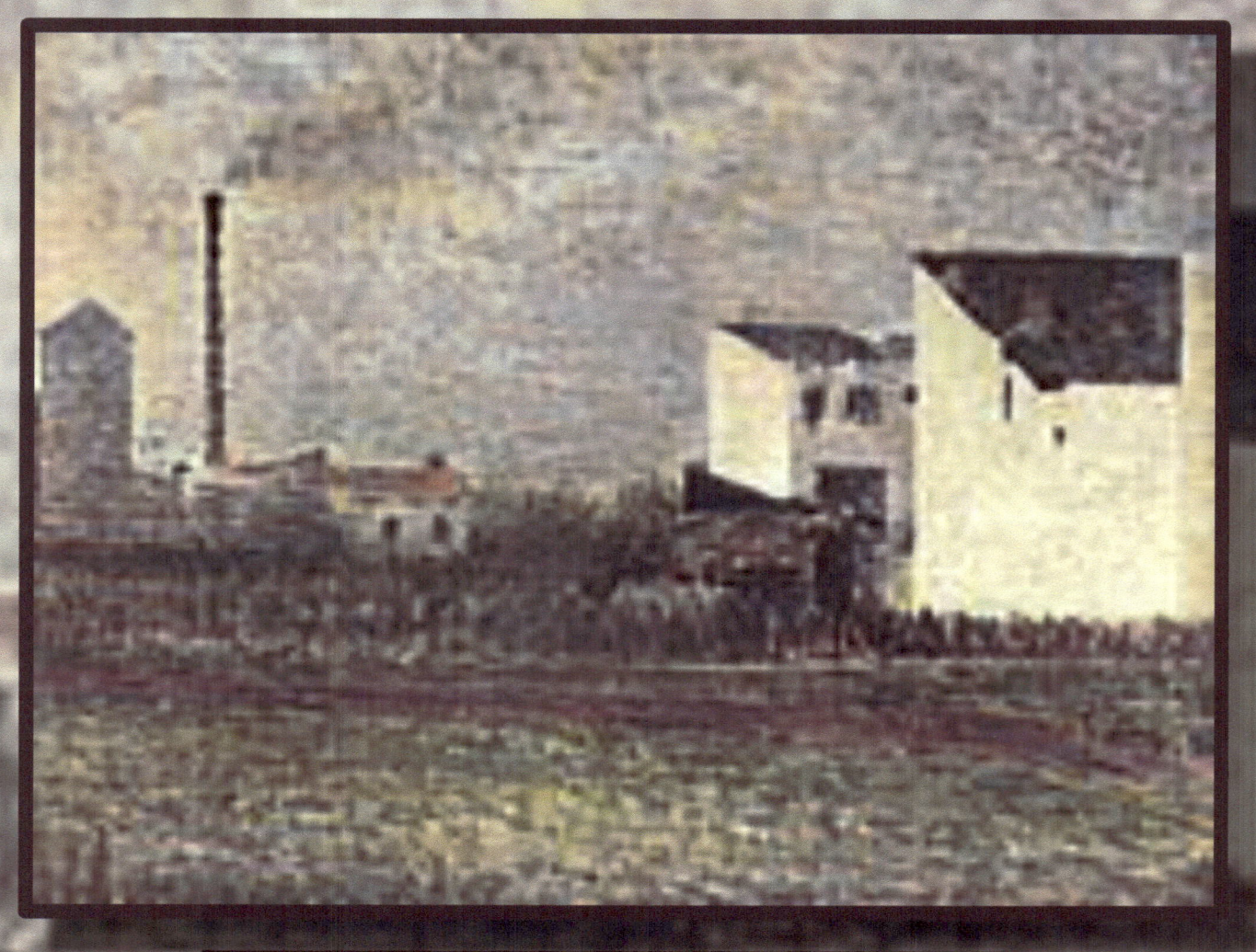

The Suburbs
1882–83, Musée d'art moderne de Troyes

Georges used color to create harmony and emotion in art.

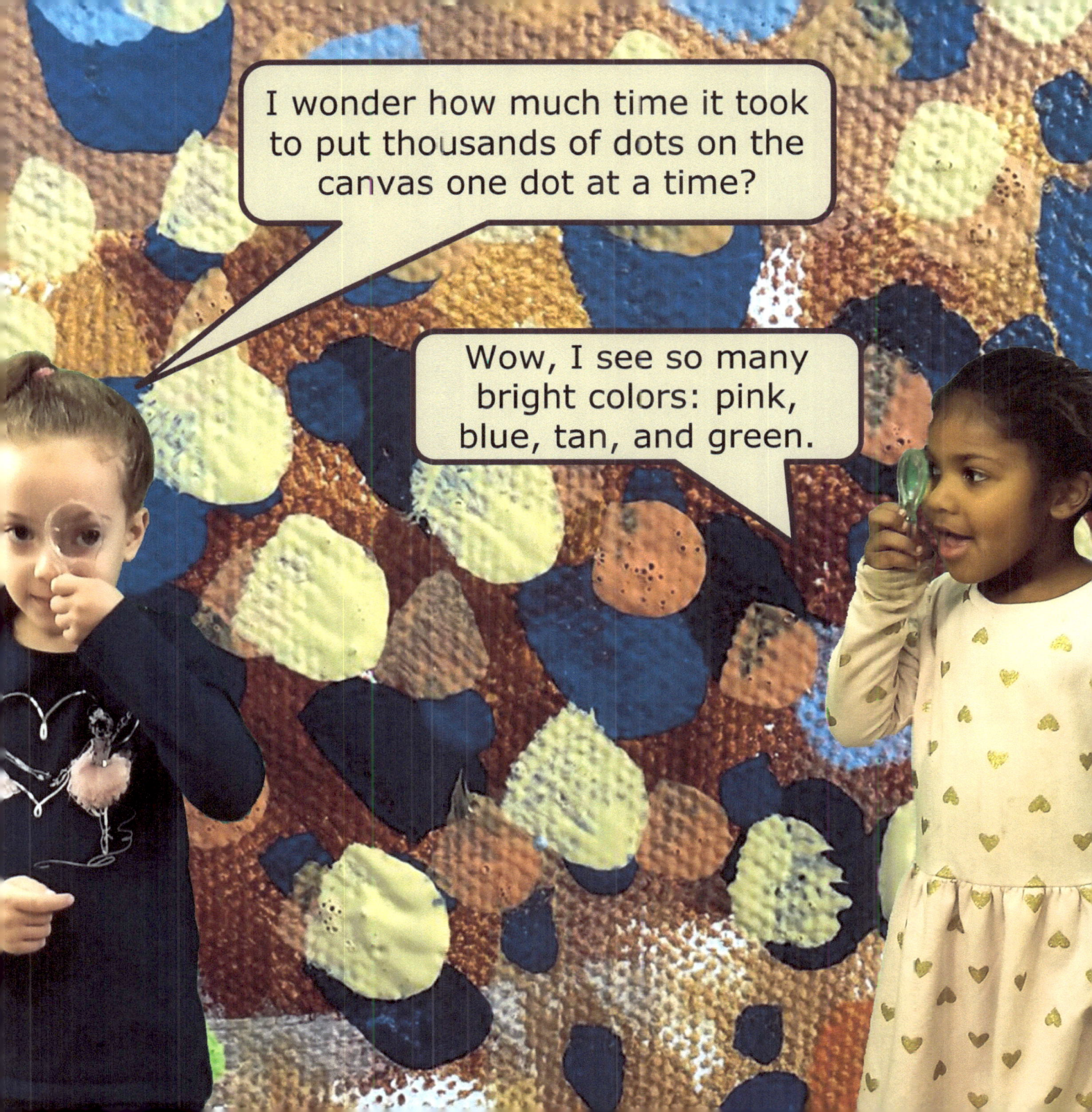

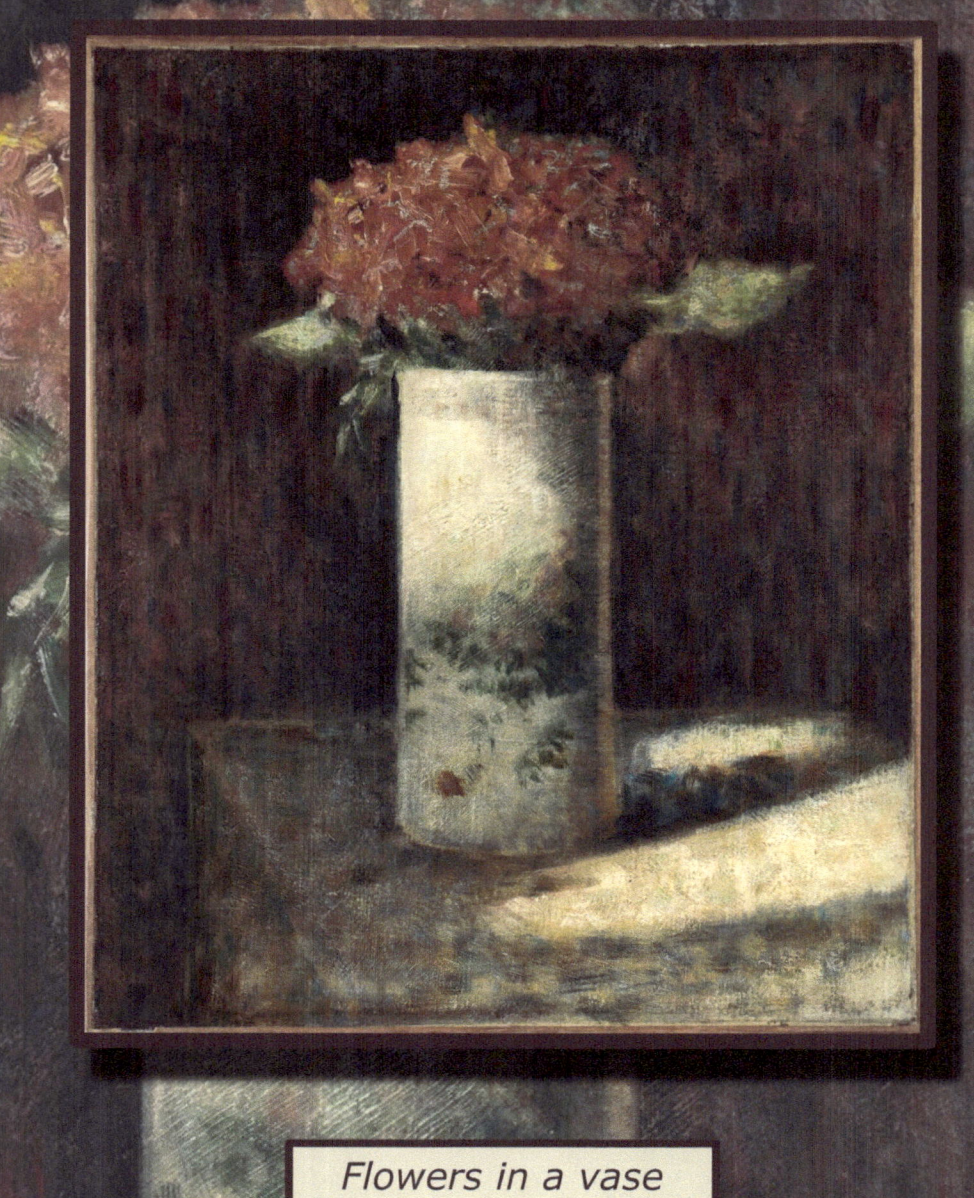

Flowers in a vase
1879, Fogg Museum

Seurat believed the process of putting colored dots on the canvas could better capture the colors of nature.

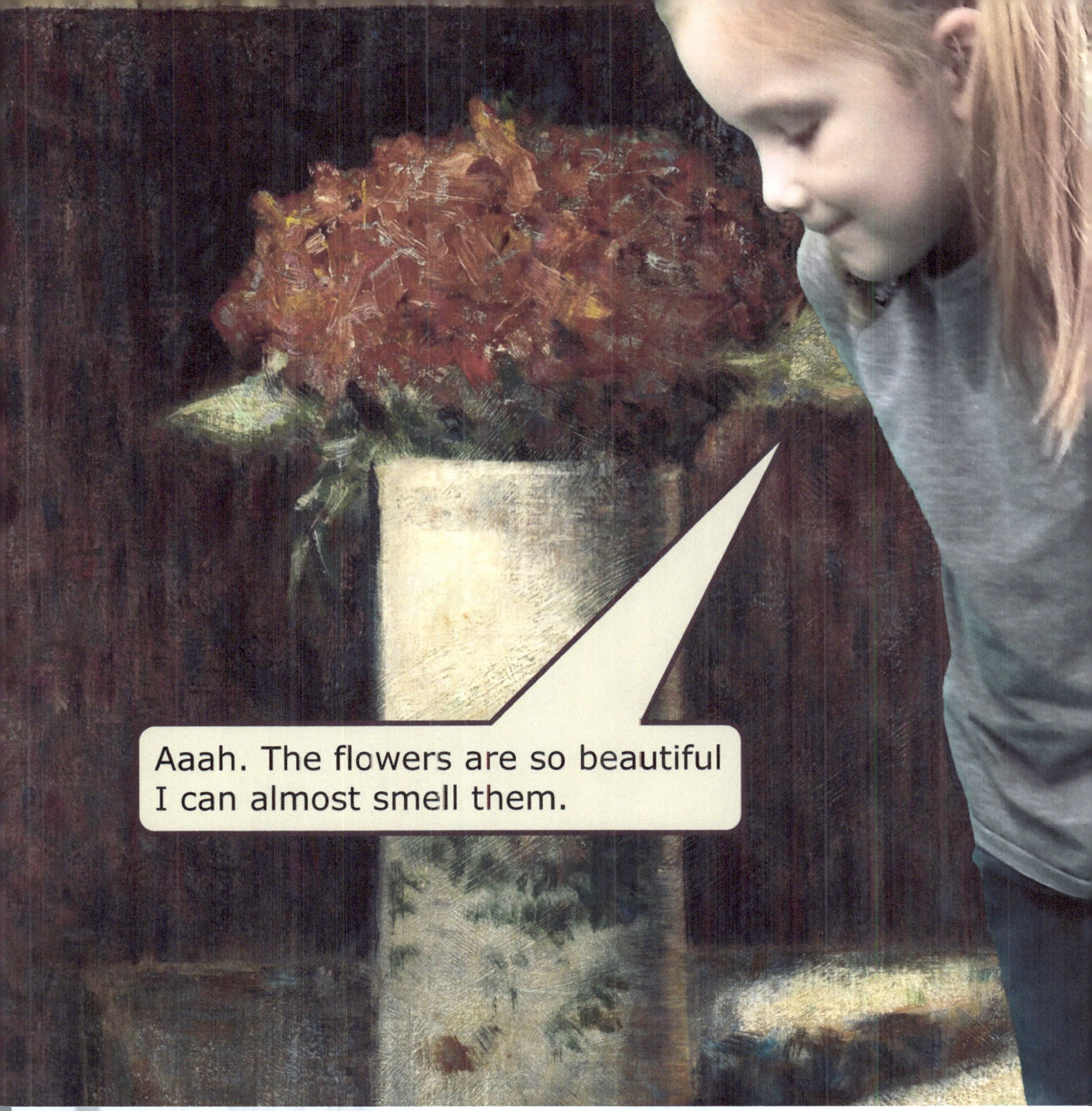

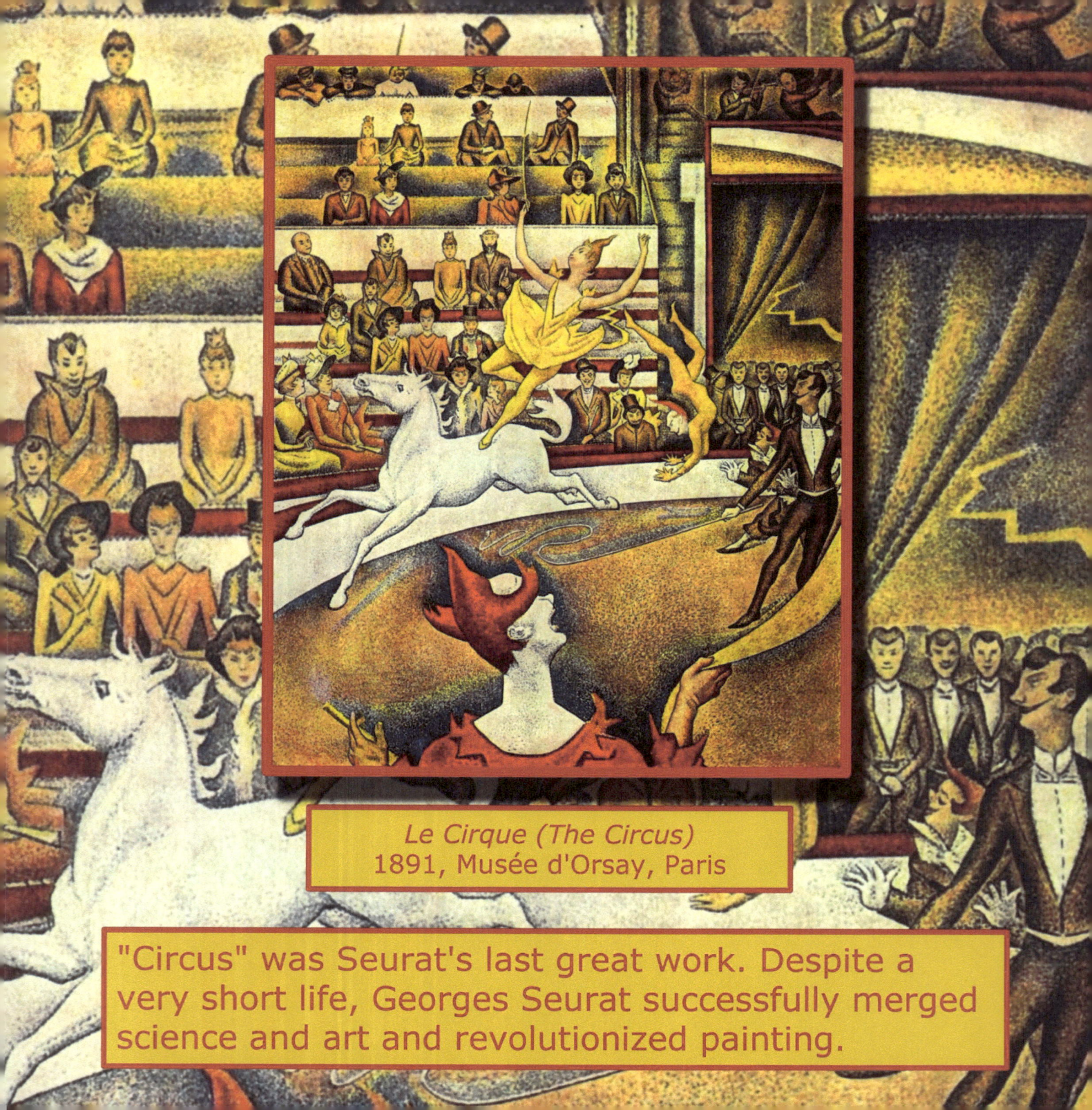

Le Cirque (The Circus)
1891, Musée d'Orsay, Paris

"Circus" was Seurat's last great work. Despite a very short life, Georges Seurat successfully merged science and art and revolutionized painting.

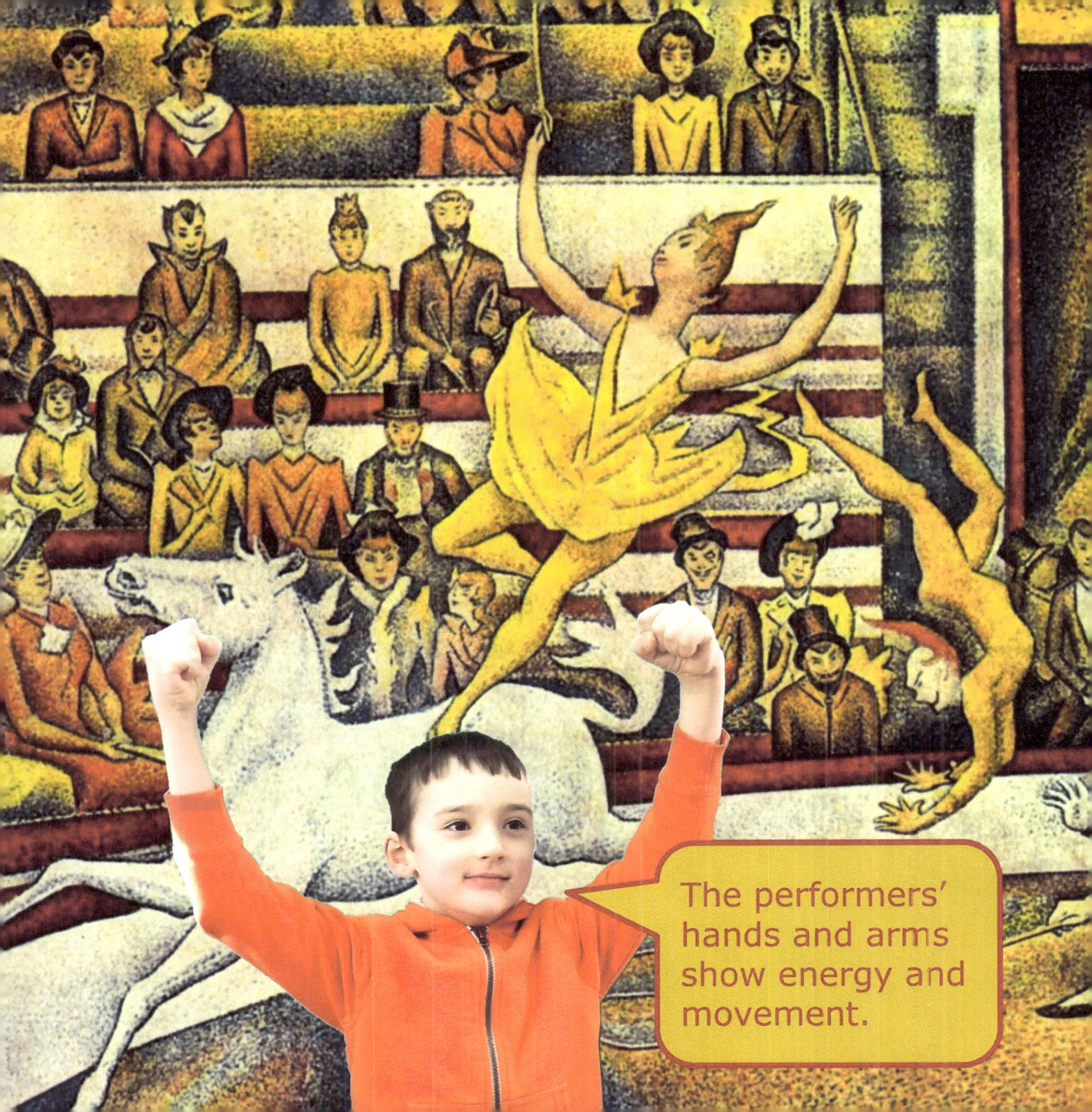

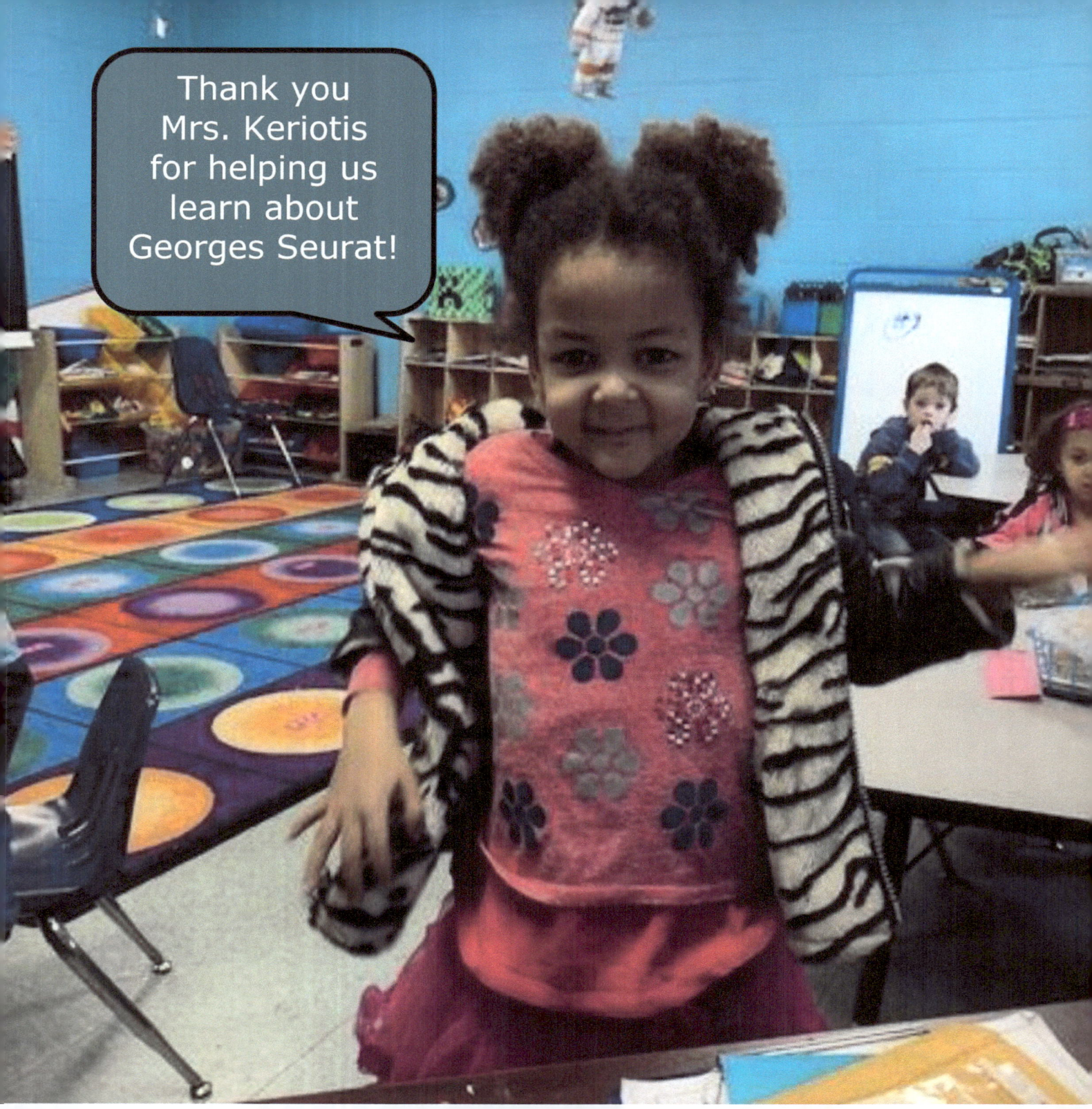

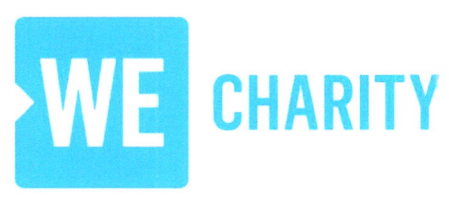

Any and all profits from this book are donated to We Charity. This amazing organization empowers communities to lift themselves out of poverty.

They do this through domestic programs like WE Schools and internationally through WE Villages. Their unique partnership with ME to WE, a social enterprise, ensures that WE Charity achieves a remarkable rate of financial efficiency, with an average of 90 percent of donations going directly to youth-serving programs.

In Canada, the US, and the UK, WE Day and WE Schools are initiatives of WE Charity that educate and empower young people. WE Schools is a yearlong educational program that nurtures compassion in students and gives them the tools to create transformative social change. And WE Day is a series of stadium-sized events that celebrate youth making a difference in their local and global communities.

Baden Academy Charter School

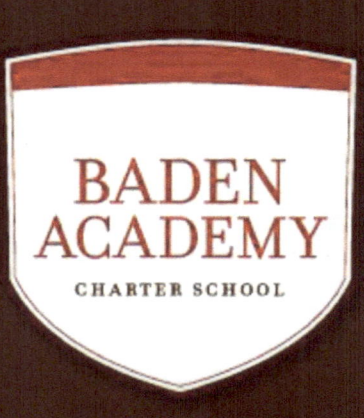

This public charter school in Western PA works to inspire personal excellence. They cultivate the inherent gifts and talents present in all children by providing a curriculum which integrates the arts and sciences in a highly interactive, hands-on environment.

Grow a Generation

Grow a Generation partners with gifted and talented young people and teachers to make meaningful projects possible. Faculty, students, and student teams apply in their school to be accepted into the fellowship program. Once selected, they embark on a year-long odyssey to publish a book, create a digital artifact, or enter a STEM competition. Find out more at growageneration.com

www.ingramcontent.com/pod-product-compliance
Lightning Source LLC
Chambersburg PA
CBHW051822210526
45473CB00005B/1697